DIRK KREUTER

New Biz Turbo Charger 4.0

- **Europe's No. 1 Sales Coach, Speaker & Business Consultant**
- **World Record 2018 for the largest sales training**
- **More than 79,000 Supervised Organizations**
- **More than 24,000 Sales and Affiliate Partners**

Apply these Rules for an Everlasting Business Success!

Dirk Kreuter
NEW BIZ TURBO CHARGER 4.0

Cover photo: Dirk Kreuter
Cover design and typesetting: Beate B. Köhler

Published by Clearsight Media, London, U.K.

1st edition
ISBN 978-1-7397779-0-6

CONTENTS

LEADERSHIP 122

FOREWORD

A warm welcome!

Have you seen the movie *Forrest Gump*? Do you remember the main character's friend, who, everywhere in the world, perceived only shrimp and thought only of shrimp? There is a scene where he spent 40 seconds listing all the variations of preparing shrimp. He was obsessed with shrimp.

It is similar to me with sales, distribution, marketing, leadership, and motivation. Everywhere in everyday life, I encounter situations from which I design creative tips for salespeople or derive motivational stories for sales. The people in my circle know this: I suddenly get all quiet and thoughtful... And then my friends know that I'm busy developing another story for my readers. This gives me great pleasure and surely for you as well!

You can read the book from beginning to end. Or you can enjoy only one story every night before going to sleep. You can also use the examples to spice up your sales meetings as a manager. Each story is independent in itself. Read in the order you like best.

"A good salesperson determines the images in his customer's

mind!"... like a good author!

I wish you a lot of fun and exciting insights. Yours...

Dirk Kreuter

The colleague Dr. Reinhard K. Sprenger claims that you cannot motivate salespeople. You can only make sure that they do not become demotivated. I think there's something to that. If you are a manager, you will find some exciting ideas in the next chapter on how to protect your sales staff from becoming demotivated. Are you a salesperson yourself? Then I wish you a lot of fun and thoughtful minutes with the stories to come.

"Motivate Me, Why Don't You!" — The Difference Between Stimulus and Drive

My six-year-old son Ben has been playing for the soccer club for a year now. As a father, it is exciting to observe how the children behave. For example, during halftime: All of them are exhausted. But after a brief moment of recovery, the boys grab a ball and continue to play casually until the restart. The coach must then intervene and force the children to take a break.

Do you have to motivate six-year-olds to play soccer? Do they need a *concept of the enemy*, i.e., an opponent they want to defeat? Does the trainer have to promise a reward for good performance?

Even before Ben played in the soccer club, I could observe the phenomenon that Ben dislikes to run around senselessly. Whether going for a walk or doing a few laps with me on the sports field, he was never interested! Until a ball came into play. Then he ran to complete exhaustion. It seems to be in the boys' genes: Ball = Fun.

Let's look at the motivational psychology: A distinction is made here between extrinsic and intrinsic motivation. Or put in simpler terms: Stimulus and drive.

Stimulus means you promise your dog a sausage if he chases the rabbit out of the undergrowth. But if your dog is already tugging on the leash because he caught the scent of the rabbit, then that's the drive. (Hunting) dogs do not need to be motivated. They have a desire to do the job.

You don't have to motivate my son to play soccer. It does not need a stimulus. It is his drive to play with the ball and the other boys: Intrinsic motivation.

If you are a manager in sales, this means you need salespeople who have the drive to sell. If you have identified the right candidate in the selection process, you do not need to motivate them. They are already motivated when they start working for you. You can't actually motivate them at all. You can only promote their stimulus.

Sure, the salesperson now, figuratively speaking, still needs a ball. The ball, in this case, is the goal in sales. Goals are an important tool when managing people. It is essential in sales! Sales targets are the most important management tool for salespeople!

Mental Leap: Ben's enthusiasm for soccer matches and training has been somewhat dampened for the past few weeks. Many boys are changing clubs (interesting fact: it's the talents and top performers who are changing!). Why? Because their coach is always yelling. He yells at the kids during practice and matches.

Quite often, tears flow. Most often, parents observe the scenes in bewilderment: Does it have to be like this? It is interesting to observe that the coaches of the opposing teams are much calmer during the Sunday tournaments!

You cannot motivate your players/employees as a coach/manager! You can only make sure that they are not demotivated!

These are the two most important sentences in this chapter!

As a manager, please ask yourself: Did you select employees with the drive for the task at hand? Do these have a ball (goals)? Do you make sure that your players can exercise their drive? Or are you demotivating your salespeople with administrative tasks that have nothing to do with the actual drive? Are you doing everything you can not to demotivate?

Another quote from Arno Schimpf, the national women's soccer team's sports psychologist, has already won the European championship title five times in a row with his team! In an interview with the magazine *Psychologie Heute*, he was asked the following question: "Then you don't encourage motivation much at all, but already assume it?" Schimpf answered, "Yes, exactly. We only nudge them once in a while and support them in decisive phases... But a high inner willingness to perform must already be present. For a top athlete, however, motivation is almost too little. It takes passion or obsession. That's what it takes to pursue a goal over ten or fifteen years because that's how long it takes in some sports to get to the top."

Do You Have a Concept of the Enemy? Or What Motivates You To Excel in Sales?

"What does someone who manufactures tractors know about sports cars!" is what Enzo Ferrari is said to have said after a customer complained about the clutch on his Ferrari 250 GT.

It was in the 60s. A wealthy entrepreneur who manufactured tractors was unhappy with several details of his sports car. But the Ferrari boss was infuriated by the criticism. So the tractor manufacturer installed a clutch in the sports car himself. A clutch for tractors!

But that was not the end of the story! Now the entrepreneur's ambition had been aroused: From now on, his goal was to build a better sports car!

The man's name? Ferruccio Lamborghini.

The competition to see who can build the best sports car continues to this day!

My conclusion: Both have the other as an enemy image. They both want to be better. They both drive each other to peak performance. Having concepts of the enemy is good for corporate development! Especially in sales!

Another example: Since 2007, I have been accompanying a company's sales team that does its business on the Internet. Today a multimillion-dollar company. Market leader. By far.

About 50 salespeople in the offline world: telemarketers and sales representatives.

In the early years, there was a clear enemy image: The market leader with American roots. The culture of the enemy image was intensively cultivated at the time. Also in my trainings. Everyone had a goal: Market leader! Everyone worked hard to displace the competitor. This has always been a lot of fun for the salespeople and me. We have tried everything!

For some time now, my customer has been the market leader. With many lengths ahead! But now the mood in sales has changed. People become much more preoccupied with themselves than is good for them. Now there are self-defined growth targets for sales orientation. But that is something quite different from an enemy image. Targets are nowhere near as motivating as having a clear concept of the enemy. Too bad. And number two has come to terms with its position. Nothing more is coming here. Yes, I would like to have a concept of the enemy again.

How is that for you? What drives you to excellence in sales?

My tip: Think about the culture of the enemy image in your market for a moment! It's worth it!

Loser!

Steve Jobs was terminated at the age of 30.

And this in the company that he had founded. He got depression and self-doubt.

Albert Einstein did not learn to speak until he was four years old. "That boy will never become anything decent," his teachers said.

Walt Disney was fired from a magazine because he had no original ideas and lacked imagination.

The Beatles were turned away from Decca Recording Studios because they didn't like the sound and it was believed that they would have no future as musicians in show business.

Thomas Edison was told by his teacher that he was too stupid to achieve anything in life.

Oprah Winfrey was fired as a news anchor, saying she was not fit for television.

The application of Andreas, a former sales trainer from my team, was rejected by the training organization of one of the largest automobile manufacturers. The reason: He is a good car salesperson, but unsuitable as a trainer. Four years after this rejection, he played a decisive role in shaping the European training concept for this manufacturer over five months. At a train-the-trainer seminar for internal trainers, one of the participants said: "We should send that one to our merchants sometime." To which his colleague replied: "Are you crazy? If that one was there, we need never come back!"

At the beginning of my sales career, based on my application, I was invited to an assessment center for candidate screening at Rank Xerox in Neuss. I admit it wasn't my best day: With a cold and fever, I still wanted to take my chance. But already after the first two exercises, one of the managers said that I wouldn't stand a chance here. I was finished. He then told me that I should consider whether sales was the right thing for me.

It's not about what happens to you. It's always about how you deal with it!

In each given example, the supposed "loser" could also have spent the night crying into his pillow before giving up with self-doubt.

You always have a choice!

Is your competitor attacking your customers? Your most important customers want to "take a break for a year" and test a new supplier? The purchasing department puts your services out to tender once again via online auction? As a sales representative, your travel area will be reduced: "Growth by cell division"? Does your boss demand a price increase in the double-digit percentage range?

And? How do you deal with it?

When Is the Best Time for Success in Sales?

Christmas Eve. During the Christmas greeting on the phone, my friend Karsten tells me that he still has a canvassing appointment on the 30th: a bank. Excuse me? On December 30?

Office day. One of my telemarketers is sitting across from me. Since I'm rarely in the office, I don't have my "own" desk. I usually join my telemarketers. It's Friday, 04:20 p.m., and I can hear him wrapping up the most important job of the week. We are both really happy about it! Most of all, about the timing! Friday… 04:20 p.m…!

October 4. It's a Friday. The bridge day after the German Unity Day. Looking back, it was the day with the highest net rate in telephone sales on my team! There were an incredible number of decision-makers on the phone that day! Often the »firewall« in the antechamber had turned the bridge day into a vacation and left the boss to his fate. At the same time, most of the conversational partners were much more approachable and willing to talk, as it was a quiet day at the desk for them as well.

When is the best time for success in sales?

TIP

Spanning across industries, an "ideal" time has emerged in recent years: The time period between the 1st of January and the 31st of December of any given year is absolutely perfect!

Conclusion: Question your beliefs! Successful salespeople do things that unsuccessful salespeople would never do!

According to What Do You Set Your Watch?

An old story: Eduard works in a factory. But he lives on the other side of town. Every morning he walks to work and stops halfway at a jewelry store. There is a beautiful old clock in the shop window, after which he sets his watch. The same ritual every day.

One day, the jeweler approaches him and inquires about what he does every morning in front of his shop window. Eduard explains that he is a foreman in the factory and is responsible for ensuring that the noon siren sounds at 12:00 p.m. on the dot. Therefore, he sets his watch every morning according to the beautiful old clock in the shop window.

To this, the jeweler replies: "That's interesting. We've been setting the clock according to your noon siren for years!"

According to what do you set your watch? According to what do you orient yourself? Many people set their watches according to the watches of others. Many people orient themselves according to the results of others. They say: "If you don't work for your own goals, you automatically work for the goals of others!"

And in sales? According to what do you orient yourself? Set your clock according to…

… what you were told was right and possible during training?
… what your manager tells you is right and possible?
… what your colleagues tell you is right and possible?
… what the press writes, what is right and possible in your market?
… what you have anchored in your mind as limiting beliefs about what is right and possible?

Especially in sales, question what is right and what is possible: Working methods, argumentation, prices, assortment, customer groups, potentials, etc.

He who does what everyone does gets what everyone gets! Welcome to mediocrity! Or: According to what do you set your watch?

Arm in Cast, Bruises, and Brasions … or: How Badly Do You Want Success?

Spring. Skatepark. My son and I. No, we do not falsify the average age: My son is usually the youngest at eight years old, and I am almost always the oldest on the board. He with his skateboard, BMX, and "tricks scooter," as he calls it, I with skateboard or longboard. A nice hobby. And ideal for conducting "social studies" among young people: What are 13- to 22-year-olds like?

A few observations that are also exciting for salespeople:

The kids practice the same trick for hours. Incredible endurance. The same movement sequence a hundred times.

90 % of all attempts fail. At least at the beginning. Later it gets better. Giving up is out of the question. The others can do the trick, too. Or anyone in a YouTube clip, which they then watch together on their smartphones during their breaks.

They observe each other. Give each other feedback without being asked. Or ask the one who is able to do it what they are doing wrong. That's quite normal. Also, for mega cool teens!

Often the attempt is filmed with the smartphone and then analyzed in the group. Naturally.

Arm in cast, bruises, and abrasions… all this is no reason to stop now. The trick has to work somehow!

Therefore… I'm sure you can guess what I'm getting at… It may be that the one or the other does not deliver good grades in school, but the basic attitude of "wanting to succeed" is clearly visible. Perhaps some teachers fail to get teens excited about their subject… This makes me think back to my school days…

How is it now with salespeople? How is that with yourself?

How often do you try a new sales technique? Take "active referral marketing," for example: This method of acquiring new customers is beyond any doubt!!! But most often, the salespeople do not ask or ask only two or three times. And then comes, "Doesn't work for me." The teens practice it until they get it right. And you?

Do you watch DVDs where a professional explains the method or technique? The teens are doing it!

Do you ask successful colleagues how they go about it? Or are you afraid to lose face? Or... do you give colleagues feedback and tips without being asked? And how do they react to this? The skaters can handle it quite naturally.

Do you role-play sales situations or practice with video feedback? Do you record your phone calls and listen to them later in a self-critical manner? That's what kids have their smartphones for!

You lose a few customers and/or jobs, and then you know that this is not the way to do it? The price is too high, the competition too strong, the customers too stupid, your product not good enough? And then? Vale of tears and "service by the book"? Skaters practice even with an arm in a cast!

My tip: Go to a skatepark sometime when the weather is nice. Observe. Think about how you learn and develop today!

Skaters do it all for fun... You and your family make a living from it!

Salesperson? Yes. Always?

Summer 2012. My kids invited their elementary school and kindergarten friends to a pool party in our backyard. The parents drop their children off with me and leave their cell phone numbers in case of an emergency. But a father hands me his business card directly with the note: "Oh, and if you ever need a bankruptcy advisor, feel free to call me!" A nice conversation developed from this, although I informed him that my business development is definitely developing positively and that I am sure that I am far from the subject of insolvency. "Well..." he said, "... if not with you, maybe you know someone..." that came across as very nice, likable, and with a smile.

Later on, when he picked up his daughter, we immediately had an interesting small talk topic. I wanted to know which companies he was working for and what exactly he was doing there. Interesting! Very interesting!

What impressed me: He is a salesperson! And his canvassing work doesn't end on a Friday afternoon in the office; he lives his profession with passion! He always canvasses when the opportunity arises. He is convinced of what he does and if I don't need it, I might know someone for whom his service is interesting. Keyword "referral marketing". Of course, it's not what you say but the way you say it! His question struck me as quite sympathetic and natural. I like that!

How about you? Salesperson? Yes. Always?

In my team, the philosophy is that we also approach our suppliers about our offer or offer our services to visitors and callers who want to sell us something or identify the need. This has already led to a number of jobs and many recommendations.

Everyday life is full of (sales) opportunities! Use them!

Not: "Money makes the world go round!" — rather: "Sales makes the world go round!"

How Persistent Are You?

Do you know the Brazilian writer Paulo Coelho? His most famous work is *The Alchemist*. This book almost faded into insignificance because its publisher had withdrawn the work from the program. Just under 1,000 copies had been sold. Coelho could have left it at that, and we would never have known about it. But the author looked for another publisher who marketed the book more successfully: To date, it has been translated into 62 languages and sold nearly 30 million copies.

Paulo Coelho was confident in his work. And he was persistent. This persistence is a characteristic of many successful people: I spontaneously think of Steve Jobs and Dieter Bohlen. In the biography of Steve Jobs, you will find scenes where he refuses to leave the client's meeting room in negotiations if the client does not respond to his proposal! Or Dieter Bohlen, who kept sending the music producers his demo tapes in his early years.

All of them mentioned have in common that you simply do not accept failure!

> "People always blame circumstances for what they
> are. I don't believe in circumstances. The people
> who go ahead in this world always go out and look

for the circumstances they need and create them when they can't find them."
George Bernard Shaw (1856-1950), Irish author

What does this mean for sales?

Do you accept "no" as an answer during cold calling? Or do you call back later? Or send a personal letter or the checklist with "10 points to look out for when buying...!" ("Geistige Brand-stiftung®", [Mental Arson]) in the follow-up.

Rotate the buyers on the job: At Aldi, a buyer only ever has to deal with a salesperson for a maximum of six months. Then the contact persons deliberately change so that no personal relationships influence the negotiations! Is your contact person still in their position with your target customer? Stay on the ball!

TIP: Are your customers or target customers on XING? Then get in touch there. As a Premium member, you should look at this feature once a month: power search "Direct contacts whose company/position has recently changed". Here you can conveniently see who has changed companies or areas of responsibility. I always have a follow up in my calendar around the 15th of the month where I am reminded of this research function.

But even without XING, it makes sense to internalize the following philosophy:

3P: Polite persistence pays!

... and with That, We Are Miles Away from Closing the Sale Right Now — or: Why Salespeople Need to Trust Themselves!

This week we had a salesperson visit our office to sell us a big — a really big — investment. We had invited him. We asked him directly. We also have concrete needs. And: He also still happens to come by way of a referral! He has already made great strides in advance in preparation for this appointment, even without an order!

The conversation and his proposal presentation were good. The product offered also meets our expectations and wishes. Everything seems to fit.

But something made me feel uneasy. The sales professional in me kept noticing hesitation in the salesperson. So along the lines of: Surely there must be an objection here now. Why aren't they asking critical questions here?

My gut was telling me: Something is not right here. Do not decide on anything just yet. Review his statements in retrospect. Research! And that's what I'm doing right now. I have already had three phone calls with people from my network who confirm my critical stance. And with that, we are miles away from closing the sale right now!

A dog can tell if the mailman is scared. Accordingly, the dog bites or not.

A horse senses whether or not the rider feels confident in the jump. The reaction to this can be denial.

As customers, we feel whether a salesperson stands behind his offer, his products, his company, his profession and his prices — or not. And when in doubt, we prefer not to buy.

Convincing customers is much more complex than just determining needs, arguing benefits and closing techniques: Decisions to buy are made emotionally — to justify them rationally later!

Salespeople need maximum self-confidence. In themselves as human beings. As a person. And in their activity. I have to trust myself as a salesperson — otherwise, the customer won't either!

Self-confidence comes from within. I have to be clear about doing my thing. What I have decided to do myself.

Are you that confident salesperson who appears to the customer in a way that leaves no room for doubt?

Hard Work Pays Off — Nothing Comes from Nothing: Hit Rate and Impact in Sales

"One-sixth of all working people in a developed economy are employed in sales and distribution. Many of them are in the field or are entrepreneurs. And they all have one thing in common: They can all sell more than they have sold so far! How can a salesperson sell more and more and more? The best salespeople have clear principles that they follow steadily and consistently."

Prof. Dr. Karl Pinczolits

Last year it was "my book of the year" that I read: *Der Schlag-zahlmanager* [The Hit Rate Manager] by colleague Pinczolits. Because… I have paid more and more attention to "quality" in sales. Since the book, I have also paid much more attention to "quantity" in sales activities. And… it works… for my team and me — but also in many customer projects — we can significantly increase success via "quantity"!

Professor Pinczolits will therefore appear from time to time in this book. Here with the first two of five salesperson principles:

1. **Working hard daily**
   "Hard work pays off" is an old saying that is especially import-ant in sales. Customer contacts and time are the basis and starting point for any sales success. One of the key findings from research in sales is: Those who do more ultimately get more out of it. The simple explanation for this phenomenon is that as the number of contacts with customers increases, so do new and additional business opportunities. This expands the opportunity base and thus the options, and the salesper-son can select the best opportunities from a larger potential. Activity is the basis for success. Higher frequency results in more business and many contacts bring many contracts. The questions that are posed here are: "How much must you do?" and secondly: "What do you have to do?" to be successful in sales. Activities, let's call them "hit rates", follow specific laws, cannot be saved in a file and as a rule you can't catch them up. Managing your activities is the be all and end all of all successful sales. Growing in a market means either more activity with customers (hit rate), more productivity (impact)

or higher selling quality (success rate). Here increasing the hit rate is the base and the simplest way to increase market pressure.

Inactive salespeople who only wait for customer reactions will always have difficulty in sales. The first indicator for inactivity is the percentage of working time that the salesperson spends on selling. We know that in almost all industries, the time that field staff, for example, actually spend with customers is around 30% and that another 30% is spent on administration. Increasing the "eye to eye" working time, and the associated increase of the contact rate, leads to the possibility of expanding opportunities."

2. Backing the right horse

Professionals distinguish between tasks and activities. They avoid treating them equally, because not every activity brings the same success, and often sales success is increased by simply changing the order in which activities are carried out. Professionals increase their productivity by concentrating on the important tasks and trying to increase the share of those in their overall activity. Increasing the hit rate has a far more profound effect on customers and market than a purely additive growth in activities would make you suspect. Firstly: They get better at everything that they do more often. A higher hit rate improves the quality of their actions. Secondly: A high hit rate broadens professional opportunities and options. A high hit count ensures success, and results increase out of proportion with the hit rate. Thirdly: Essential tasks become easier, because everything that people do more often becomes easier for them.

What is the most important hit rate? Of the several thousand activities that a salesperson does on average over the course of his or her life, there are a few that are largely responsible for his success. These are the "key hit rates". A key hit rate can be many things: A test drive at the car dealership, a consultation at the bank, a demonstration on the construction site, a quotation in the investment business. An analysis of top salespeople shows a high percentage of key hit rates compared to total activity.
If you concentrate on the essentials, you must never do the wrong work. The wrong sales activities are often proven productivity thieves.
Anyone who backs the right horse daily will achieve up to thirty percent yield in opportunity on his number of contacts. Anyone who limits wrong and unproductive activities, and contact with unproductive customers, to less than 20% of his working time has a better activity/result ratio."

100x as Productive—30 to 40x as Efficient—Every Salesperson Can Sell More than They Are Actually Selling

... I now owe you the three missing principles of success for salespeople from Prof. Dr. Karl Pinczolits that I announced in the last story... Here we go:

3. Taking a clear step

"Those who make quick and clear-cut decisions every day are more productive in sales. The most important decisions you have to make are: which customers will be looked after with which products or services. Becoming more productive means carrying out the right activities with the best customers. You could work six times harder than the worst salesperson in your sector, but you could be a hundred times as productive if you approach the right customers with the right products.

Selling to the best customers means that you consciously select your target group daily. Productivity means distinguishing valuable customers from less valuable customers and then looking after them correspondingly. The number of right activities at the right time with your customers and markets is the key to higher productivity here. Professionals never look after the wrong customers. Contacting the right customers in the right time window can be thirty to forty times as effective as coincidental or unplanned sales pitches. But the right timing is also important — for example, if customers are given the price at the end of the selling process, higher prices can be achieved."

4. Hitting the nail on the head

"Our fourth starting point at your disposal to influence professionalism is the specific sales act or deal. The question here is, how do you speed up each business case and improve your success rate? The central skill here is acting quickly and simply. The aim here is to rationalize the development of sales activities from the first contacts with customers to a long-term business relationship. The longer, the more intensive the manipulation, the more complicated a single selling action is, the lower the productivity. You'll achieve a high deal flow (number of closings, orders, in the time unit) if you manage to look after customers quickly and easily. Customers also admire people more if they're seen to process many sales acts quickly and easily.

If you sell in a cumbersome and complicated way, you will soon have problems in managing your business because dealing with the volume of business simply consumes too much time and energy. Salespeople with a high deal flow can oversee double as many customers and also double as many business deals in the same time as other, average, salespeople."

5. Taking responsibility increases your selling performance

Your own work organization, self-control and self-efficacy are further keys to increasing your performance. You use your manpower optimally when you are neither under-challenged nor overburdened. Good self-control increases productivity, as you turn market opportunities into doable activities. Never not having a plan means that you turn opportunities into results.

If you enter a market without planning and preparation, your sales activities will be uncoordinated and you will not achieve your goals, or you'll only achieve them with a lot of stress. If you convert goals into activities and plan them, for example, you are three times more likely to hit your target than without having planned. Appropriate self-organization allows you to reduce your working time and avoid bottle-necks, and to pay attention to the correct mix of individual activities. Years ago, salespeople had time to become productive. These days they often require you to bring in more than you cost in the first year already.

Every salesperson can sell more than they are actually selling. This applies to salespeople as well as business owners who sell. The difference between the actual and the possible performance is called the performance gap. The personal performance gap is between 20 and 30% for every salesperson.

If you concentrate on the factors described, you'll sell more in a shorter time and with less personal effort.

"More appropriate activities, at the best customers with the right products, fast and easy, well-organized and -planned!" Only in this way, and in no other way, can you sell professionally like a world champion. The opposite of this claim just doesn't work. "A salesperson who looks after unimportant customers with the wrong actions, seldom and without planning and at the wrong time, is guaranteed not to have success!"

By the way: Should you as salesperson fill up or wash your car between two customer visits? No way!!! Do you know how many sales opportunities you miss out on with a few thousand salespeople going about their daily business? How much turnover is NOT generated by doing that?

That Which Brought You This Far Will Not Take You Further

A double door at the airport. The man in front of you holds the door open for you. You thank him politely. At the next door you reciprocate and hold the door open for him. You see things like that every day. Quite normal. Done unconsciously. The expert term for this phenomenon: The principle of reciprocity. Or put in simpler terms: The debt of gratitude.

We experience this effect in many areas of our lives. Yet, how can you use this phenomenon to your advantage in sales?

A few years ago, a sect optimized this effect to such an extent that it "acquired" large sums of money: They positioned themselves mainly at airports and train stations and greeted travelers very warmly while giving them a flower. This was followed by the request for a donation. The success rate was enormous. And now you know why the yield was so high.

A study on the tipping of waiters found that tipping is about 20% higher when the waiter presents the check together with free candy.

How often do we use something in which the first month, the first hour, or whatever, is free. And then stay with it. Out of gratitude. Because we think it wouldn't be fair otherwise…

Implementation? Is it tangible now? I like to give target customers a suitable book as a gift. With a dedication and explanation in an accompanying letter. I usually find an individual »hook« about the company or the person in a press article. The book "What brought you this far will not take you further: How successful people become even more successful" is a good fit for a target customer who is not willing, despite intensive objection handling, to compare his supplier with what I can offer. The title of the book already tells him what I want from him. If you want to bestow even more sales on your target customer with your products or services, the book title *Extreme Sales* might be appropriate. For the topic of purchasing processes, cost optimization, opportunities for saving, the bestseller *Purchasing: grave of billions — Purchasing, the top responsibility of the entrepreneur, not only in difficult times* may be a good fit.

You have to be very creative here. If you find a book that matches what you offer, you can always gift it again and again. It's a different recipient every time!

What happens on the customer side? A book has a totally different status to a sales letter. Throwing a book into the waste basket requires willpower! You are signaling to the recipient that you have made an effort to find out about them and their work. You show interest. At the same time, you have invested in them. Books cost money. In many cases, you'll get feedback from the recipient within one or two weeks. Even CEOs say thank you with a personal letter! I've seen all this before! And then... Then you have a brilliant introduction for a follow-up conversation in a completely different mood than you may have already experienced in the initial canvassing.

You Have to Understand That Quality and Success Are Independent of Each Other . . .

Better products and services? Better prices? Or better salespeople?

If you've been to my presentations or seminars, you'll be familiar with one of my favorite quotes:

"We don't lose orders to better products, better services or better prices. We lose orders to better salespeople!"

I am totally convinced of this! And again and again I find evidence for the following statement:

"You have to understand that the quality and success of a film are independent of each other. Basically: Any film can be a success at the box office if it's marketed properly. Whereas even bad films find their audience if they are sold properly." The successful actor Will Smith in *Finance Weekly*.

So: Quality or sales?

Yes, I know, of course I won't necessarily get sales with a bad product. On the other hand, affordable prices and good quality do not automatically result in sales success either!

I see again and again that businesses delay the introduction of products and services because they want to offer the "perfect" one. Especially us Germans are hung up about perfection. Yes, of course "Made in Germany" stands for quality. But how many sales opportunities are wasted because perfection comes before marketing? Then salespeople explain to me before a trade fair why they don't want to present the new product at the trade fair, because it will only be ready and available three months later. And the trade fair would have been the ideal time to start sales activities. Three months after the fair your competitor has already placed their products and closed the door on you!

If Dieter Bohlen had wanted to bring his singing skills to an above-average level before releasing his first song, he would not have had any media sales today. But Bohlen is a genius salesperson!

The Question That the Most Ambitious Salespeople Ask Themselves

»Man has three ways of acting wisely: first, by thinking, which is the noblest, second, by imitating, which is the easiest, and third, by experience, which is the most bitter.« (Confucius)

How can I (quickly) become (even) more successful in sales/ selling? That is THE question that occupies ambitious salespeople the most. How do I find a "short-cut" to success, without having to have all the "bad" experiences myself first, and at the same time also save a whole lot of time?

How do children do it? Regardless of their age: Children model themselves on examples. On their parents to start with, later on on their older siblings, on friends, on their peers, and then in puberty on singers, film stars and sporting heroes. My seven-year-old son is not Ben when he plays football, but rather the FC Bayern goalkeeper Manuel Neuer.

I used to have a few stars on the competitive sports scene as role models. I trained like them! I used the material they used (when I could afford it). I wanted to know what their life circumstances were, I was looking for direction.

And? Yes, it worked well in many areas. And it went faster than if I'd tried it all out myself!

As a trainer and speaker, Tom Peters was my first example, my orientation, my benchmark. I was not only interested in what he wrote, but also in what was written about him. The book *The Tom Peters Phenomenon* was a wonderful inspiration for me back in 1998 already.

And you as a salesperson? Find the right examples for you: successful colleagues in your own team, successful sales colleagues in the industry or even those who are with the competition! Look to exchange ideas! Examine other people's success!

Here, there's one thing that is very important: It's not about copying someone else completely. It's much rather about taking a closer look at the area that is relevant to you, the one where you want to be even better!

Lance Armstrong is an example to me. But only in one specific area! No, it's not doping and honesty.

Also important: People who have already died can also be examples for you! Steve Jobs offers me exciting orientation options in many areas!

You don't need to know your example personally either: If you are a car salesperson, Joe Girard would probably be a good example for you. It can be demonstrated that he was the most successful car salesman on this planet.

Or if you're a financial services provider: Chris Gardner, Reinfried Pohl and Carsten Maschmeyer could be good role models for you.

If you don't know your examples personally, then at least the people mentioned above offer you their knowledge and experience in books. The Internet, too, often has a whole range of information. By reading about them, you have the opportunity to deal with their approaches and actions in peace and quiet and to shape your personal motivation on them.

What Do James Bond and My Son's Friend Have in Common?

The mobile phone rings. "Bond, James Bond…" London is at the other end of the line. A new mission. Bond accepts it immediately. Goes to work at once.

That's how it always is. In all the 007 films. Bond accepts every order, every situation. Or have you ever heard him argue as in: "Nah, not right now. I'm a bit busy at the moment. The beautiful blonde. The tasty Martini. Isn't it the rainy season in Asia now? I don't have my vaccination card with me. Don't I need a visa for there?" No, Bond is always able to and always wants to. A very special internal attitude!

Hmmm. This might be true for a special agent at Her Majesty's command. Or a character in a novel. But in everyday life?

This week, I went to an amusement park with my son Ben (7) and his friend Efe (7). Climbing and skill parkour. Both decided to go on the most difficult version of the course. Efe is much smaller than Ben and wore sandals instead of trainers. Ben had done the distance a few times before. Home advantage. It was Efe's first time there.

And what did I witness? Regardless of how difficult the task, the obstacle, the distance was: Efe never hesitated, no talking back, no complaining or anything of the sort. And he had a lot of fun as well! I recognize the "James Bond attitude" again.

So how is this relevant to sales? How many salespeople do you know (including the one that you see in the mirror in the morning) that have this "special internal attitude"? I need to think about it for a while!

Especially in sales, people love to whine, moan and nag. And, "while the intellectuals discuss the strategy, the dumbos have stormed the ramparts already!" But this is not about (sales) intelligence. This is about your own approach, your own inner attitude. Or do you think that "one" cannot be successful in sales now in mid-summer, it being holiday time?

When you think about your sales targets in future, ask yourself whether you can learn something from Efe and James Bond after all.

Million Dollar Sunday — Where Do Top Salespeople and Their Managers Get Their Ideas and Motivation From?

A few years ago, I was a participant at a four-day international conference in the USA. On the Sunday, the *Million Dollar Sunday* event took place. A small conference with 34 guests within the larger event with its 1,800 participants. Only people who could prove that they had a turnover of more than a million dollars from presentations and courses were allowed to participate. The organizer had looked at the balance sheets of the participants beforehand and, if necessary, consulted with their tax consultants. That, too, made it an exclusive little circle on that Sunday.

Each guest knew beforehand already who would be present in the circle. Everyone received "homework" before the event: you had to suggest two "Million Dollar" ideas to the other participants. Two thoughts on how one could earn or save a million dollars — in three minutes max!

Needless to say, these two ideas needed to be extraordinary! Because all the participants played in the Champions League! Nobody wanted to embarrass themselves.

This was followed by a prominent surprise guest from the business world, who reported on his inside knowledge for more than an hour, and also a practice report from a participant.

Even the breaks were exciting: Amazing contacts and exchange of ideas on the highest level!

Since then, I've made sure not to miss a single *Million Dollar Sunday*! This one day is of immeasurable value to me professionally!

So where do you get YOUR new ideas, stimuli and motivational push from?

Mobile Motivation Trainer: Advantage Arguments in Sales Using the Example of Porsche

Customers don't buy brands, they only buy their advantages!

Yet salespeople mostly talk far too much about brands and product properties instead of showing the customer what they really get with the product: Instead of talking about 480PS, Porsche forcefully pushes the advantages of its new imported model variant of the 911.

It's worth your while to drive a new 911, because …

… a Porsche has such a typical silhouette that even elderly women with visual and mobility impairments crossing the street can recognize in good time: a fast car is coming!

… when you buy a Porsche, you easily contribute $10,000 to VAT, which the state can then add to its social budget.

… it's a waste of resources to drive another brand of car that has already lost 40% in value just after it's driven off the dealer's floor.

… by acquiring it, you ensure that there will still be desirable classic cars on the market in 30 years.

… Porsche drivers are mobile motivation trainers who, while driving past, make it clear to young people why it's worthwhile to go beyond the call of duty in their occupations.

… 911 drivers have learned to make do with the essentials in life with the storage space available to them.

… in a Porsche, even top managers waive having a servant drive the car for them.

… Porsche drivers provide traffic education and remind many other vehicle drivers that there is also a right-hand lane.

What Is a Bestseller?

Larry Winget is a star on the American speaker scene. An incredible guy! In a presentation before trainers and speakers he explains, in his unique way, what a bestseller is: a book that is mentioned on an official bestseller list! That is the only thing that counts!

A number 1 in a sub-category on Amazon is not a bestseller, he made it clear at the time. Amazon is a retailer, a dealer — albeit a very large one — nothing more! And those rankings at Amazon are generated anew every hour. That has nothing to do with bestsellers.

Larry Winget knows what he's talking about: He's had a few books on the *New York Times* bestseller lists!

The reactions of the attendees to this statement were quite "fascinating"! You must know that in this industry almost everyone has written a bestseller at some time or another ;-)

For me, this presentation was the trigger for the goal: Bestseller list! I'd already achieved the Amazon sub-category number 1 position a few times…

It's come this far: Buchreport, which collects the figures for the two official bestseller lists (*Spiegel* and *manager magazine*) in Germany, have published their rankings: *Extreme Sales* is number 18 on the list of business bestsellers!

Yoohoo:-)

… and thank you, dear readers!

I am very happy about this indirect compliment!

Moved

A big advantage of my profession is that my customers often invite several speakers to their events, and in this way, I have the opportunity again and again to fill up with new knowledge myself and enjoy the performances of my colleagues at the same time. Due to the large number of other lectures and also because I've met most of my colleagues before, I am not one to quickly get enthusiastic anymore. Yet, a while ago I was privileged to experience a highlight, although it didn't look like one to start with...

The ninth fireside chat of the "Competence Partners". By invitation only. Venue: the exclusive Japanese golf club Kosaido in Düsseldorf. One of two presentations: "Gmund — a paper brand on the move", presented by the managing shareholder Florian Kohler.

I had expected a classic business presentation: Number of employees, turnover, history, foundations... in short: the usual.

After twenty minutes I was excited. Even better: moved. Not so much by the contents: it was about the fine print. More about Mr. Kohler's enthusiasm for his product, his business, his passion.

I experience many well-crafted presentations. This was also very well crafted. But you can feel the difference between someone making a presentation because they've been asked to do it, or because they earn their "daily bread" by doing it. And you notice when someone just opens a window and lets you have a glance into their life. That is what Mr. Kohler did with his presentation, and he got to the guests, and to me. He moved us!

- **Conclusion 1**

  At yesterday's internal meeting, we decided to move away from consistent digital communication with our customers and to communicate more on paper. We now "package" the quotation system, in particular, differently.

- **Conclusion 2**

  You and I, as customers, can detect whether someone wants to sell us something or whether they are a "convinced criminal". Are you and/or your team doing it out of full conviction and passion? Your performance doesn't have to be perfect. However, "call of duty" does not lead to (sales) success.

This makes me think of another story from my first year doing field sales: A new customer had placed a huge first order with me. Weeks after the order he casually gave me feedback: "Your products, dear Dirk, are indifferent. We could have got them somewhere else also. However, you were so "on fire" for your offer, your products and your company. You were so enthusiastic that it was contagious. We bought because of you."

Maybe you're thinking now that your products and services are not that emotional? That your customers are "cool operators" who make rational decisions?

I am convinced: In most cases, we lose orders to better (and more enthusiastic) salespeople!

He Who Whines, Gets Replaced!

Saturday afternoon at the football pitch. My eight-year-old son's team is playing a match. F-Youth — this is the phase in which children learn that it's not only about always running after the ball, but it's about positional play as well.

Two players started to whine about some "framework conditions" during warm-up. Everyone on the football grounds heard the coach's reply: "If you whine, you get replaced!"

And? Yes, it works! The children concentrate on the game, and this time they won 3:1.

So how is this relevant to sales?

Do salespeople really believe that if they moan about whatever and complain — about the weather, market conditions, internal problems, evil competitors etc. — when visiting customers, the customer will buy more out of sympathy? No, on the contrary: Having things in common generates sympathy, which means that the customer often gets into the topic and things are often even worse in his case! Soon you both find yourselves in the valley of tears. And we know that no business is done in the valley of tears!

TIP

**Regardless of what you've experienced —
how you are — how you feel:
CUSTOMERS ONLY BUY FROM WINNERS!
Be prepared!**

"Well... should I pretend to the customer? I want to be authentic!" Counter-question: Do you want to sell something? Don't you think that it's more likely that customers will buy (more) from you if they're in a good mood and optimistic?

There are so many customers that buy something in spite of the salesperson! Don't ever belong to that species of salesperson! Take the sales wisdom that "everything you say to the customer must be true" to heart. But you don't have to say everything that is true.

Farmers' rule: Happy cows give more milk!

Social acquisition rule: You don't kiss pessimists!

Sales rule: Customers only buy from winners!

Show Me a Sector with Lots of Resistance— and I'll Show You Salespeople Who Earn a Lot of Money!

After a presentation a participant wants to speak to me personally: "Everything you say is true, Mr. Kreuter. But it's quite difficult in my industry!"

Difficult customers. Difficult products. Difficult regions. It's difficult internally. Price war and so on...

Is that really so? Or does it have something to do with your own attitude, your own perspective?

1. "If it were easy, everyone would be doing it!"
    If there were no demanding customers/products/regions,
    nobody would need salespeople.

2. Advisors, writers, customer visitors, distributors of goods,
    discount givers don't "earn" a lot of money, do they! The
    greater the challenges, the greater your income!

3. Growth is about resistance! A muscle only ever grows after
    encountering resistance that it's not used to! Good salespeo-
    ple develop at the hand of resistance.

4. In the film *The Pursuit of Happiness* there is a scene in
    which a gospel choir sings: "Don't give me fewer problems
    and cares, but give me the strength I need to manage these
    problems better!" What do many salespeople do? They yearn
    for discounts, other areas, other products, easy customers
    and weak competitors. Does it not make more sense to work
    at your own strengths in these situations? To develop your-
    self further?

The participant mentioned at the start is the owner of a printing company. Comparable products. Price competition. Internet
suppliers. My tip in this short conversation: He should develop

"Geistige Brandstiftung®" [Mental Arson] as a checklist for his customers. A few days later he sent me the 10-point list that would make his customers think. It works! Not always. But very often! And it's fun ;-)

He won't be able to change anything about the market. But he CAN change how he reacts to it. And how do you react to your "challenges"?

And: I get around. I get profound insight into many businesses and industries every year. Please believe me: I don't see any real differences between customers in Styria, Lake Constance, Münsterland, Ruhr area, Tegernsee or Holland!

"Every Salesperson Needs This Sense of Achievement to Carry On!"

My son needed almost an hour to get the front wheel of his BMX onto the obstacle for the first time. One hour corresponds to about 30 attempts and one fall that really hurt. Then came the most exciting observation: After he got it right the first time, it worked every other time after that! Nobody should try and tell me that it's about strength or technique. It's all in the mind! All in the mind. He proved to himself that he could do it and after that he never doubted it again!

Do you know Roger Bannister? (Yes, I know… a bold transition). He was the first person to run the mile in less than four minutes. A grandiose achievement on May 6, 1954! But even more remarkable is the fact that another 37 runners broke through the four-minute barrier in that year. And in the following year more than 300 runners! This phenomenon even has a name: The "Bannister effect"... and that's all in the mind as well!

What does that have to do with sales?

As a coach and speaker, I know that the learning curve for salespeople rises steeply when trying out new skills, strategies, tactics and formulations is coupled with a sense of achievement! Every salesperson needs this sense of achievement to carry on!

And in practice? There, new telesales agents get all the "garbage addresses", the ones that have been called X times already and where nobody would be able to sell anything! So along the lines of: "At least he can't break anything..." Well, he doesn't get to break anything, but he doesn't get a sense of achievement either! That makes your motivation drop onto basement level and also doesn't make for exploring new routes.

New telesales agents need the best leads from the very first day! If you're a manager, you must make sure that the new salespeople can celebrate successes as soon as possible!

The same goes for field salespeople: Rough diamond salespeople shouldn't be allocated run-down areas with only C and D customers so that they "can try it out first"! Also, please no tours with some "old hand" who explains the world to them during coffee trips and while picking up orders from regular customers. The emphasis here is on "some"! The "newbies" must get to know your *best* salespeople. A different professional in another region every day. This is how they become acquainted with success, see what is possible and in this way push the boundaries in their own heads.

"Once you've stepped out the closet, there are no
more boundaries."

Alphonse Allais

We Didn't Get a Warning Today!

A pharmaceutical congress with an accompanying trade fair.
My customer is represented there with a stand of 6500 sq.ft.
That night on the way to the hotel he grins happily: "We didn't
get a warning today!" I wondered about that. What was so special about that?

He explained that in his industry it was something that happened just about every day. Their direct competitors employed
eleven internal lawyers, who of course had to be used to the full.
"Normally we receive warnings on the day we set up already,"
he told me. It was less about enforcing legal violations and more
about disrupting the competition in its day-to-day business.

Wow! How's that for an industry custom! Real fighting taking place here. Let me make this clear: I don't find it appropriate nor funny — just most remarkable.

Salespeople can't even dare to forget a promotional pen with the customer. They could receive a warning for that. Crazy… how complicated is that!

So… Be glad that it hasn't come to that in your industry. Be glad that you can still concentrate on your core competence: selling.

And: I always delete contact requests from lawyers via XING immediately. I'm cautious now, having once received a warning from a lawyer I contacted after a presentation at the Marketing Club. I really don't need things like that!

Never Walk! Don't Ever Hand Your Customer to Someone Else!

Mile 10 of the marathon. Everything hurts. It's so hot. Refreshment station. Inner dialogue. "Come on, you can walk here for a few yards. It's easier to drink that way. If the cola splashes into your nose again while you're running… it burns like hell…"

Never walk!

Mile 15. It's getting worse! "Now you can walk. Just a few steps."

Never walk!

Firstly: I'm talking about the marathon that concludes a long-distance triathlon: 2.4 miles swimming, 112 miles cycling and 26 miles running. That's different to a city marathon!

Secondly: Regardless of whether it's a triathlete or long-distance runner, "Never walk!" applies to both: If you walk at 10 miles, you'll walk at every refreshment station. And for longer every time. And from 20 miles you only walk. So: "Never walk!"

This also applies to sales: How often do I argue with salespeople about customers or interested people with whom the salesperson "doesn't get along". Salespeople place their prospects of success in the hands of fate like this: "You just get people with whom you notice right away that the chemistry isn't right." Oh really? And when one gets someone like that, there is nothing "one" can do? Is that so? That means, then, that "one" is dependent on the great Salesperson God who must send you the right customers?

In plain English: Salespeople have to adjust themselves to every customer, and must get along with every customer. Period. That is our job. "Chemistry" is not an excuse.

"Never walk!" here means: A salesperson does not pass on a customer to a colleague or the boss because communication is a bit challenging. Never! If you do it once, the excuses start coming faster, and fewer and fewer customers are suddenly the right fit for you. Instead of concentrating on the customer and the solution for the problem, you consider whether this is not a candidate for your colleague rather. No, do not accept your own excuses!!

If you're a manager, you're familiar with this phenomenon: It's always the same salespeople that call you because a customer is "difficult", for whom the price must be discounted or about whom the customer suddenly wants to talk to the boss. Always the same salespeople! Always! You can only blame yourself then. It takes two to tango: One who requires it and one who allows it.

You as salesperson, think about the start of your collaboration with your top customers. What is "harmonious" right from the start? After I met my wife for the first time I also thought: "That one has a heart of stone!" Today, we're happily married.

"Demanding" customers are "like that" to other salespeople too. If you're aware of that, it follows that you need to get along with each and every customer. That is the demand on yourself and your profession.

If something then goes terribly wrong, then there is still the follow-up call with the self-incrimination: One, two days — often even a week — later you call the customer who didn't want to buy one more time: What went wrong there? What should I have done? Making yourself smaller consciously... Most of the time, the customer will now react very differently than in the previous sales pitch, in which you negotiated with them on an equal footing. Normally they will now be more approachable and listen to a sales pitch one more time. The success rate with this approach is remarkable! Of course not all salespeople must do this. Yet, what do you have to lose? You already have no orders!

The Thermostat Effect!

What happens when someone who's always broke wins millions in the Lotto or inherits them? How much money does that person still have after two or three years? Nothing. Broke once more.

What happens when someone who's always been very over-weight loses 20 or 30 pounds on a diet? How much does that person weigh in one or two years' time? Mostly as much as before the diet. Often even more!

Why is that?

It's the thermostat effect. A radiator thermostat regulates the temperature of a room. If you set it to 74 °F, the room will have an average temperature of 74 °F. If the sun shines on the window surface, the temperature will increase in the short term. The thermostat immediately reduces the heat output. If you ventilate the room, the room temperature drops for a few minutes. The heating then knows that it must supply more. That's how a radiator thermostat works.

And this thermostat effect also ensures that people who have never learnt to work with money, food or exercise properly are constantly broke or fat.

If you want to change something in the long term, you should turn your attention to the thermostat effect first! First, the "temperature" in your head must be set to "prosperous" or "slim".

I heard about this effect 20 years ago already. But I didn't take any notice. Then, in the Easter holidays of 2011, I read about it again. I then set about seeing where in my head a "temperature" needed to be optimized. I found something with presentation and training days: From 2008 to 2010 my staff and I together had sold almost the same number of training days. Sometimes ten more or ten less. OK, we did generate more revenue every year through regular price adjustments, but we were stuck at a certain level in terms of the number of days. I wanted to change that!

In the weeks that followed I contemplated an ambitious revenue target: Double!

Doubling sales? Is that realistic? Seriously? What would my staff have to say about that? Granted, they were used to things like that from me, but: Doubling? Such leaps in sales could happen in a start-up, but I've been in this profession for more than 20 years and we're talking about seven-digit amounts. How was that supposed to work?

Targets are one side of the coin. Strategy and implementation are the other side. For this, I considered a few new routes to success. It was clear to me that if we kept on doing this like we had until then, we would also only have the success that we had had until then. So something fundamental had to change.

In the last weekend of August 2011, we held our traditional strategy meeting on Mallorca with my closest staff circle. These four days were always about our direction for the next year. At the end of August, our current financial year is mostly "over". So, as the boss, I presented my new knowledge around the thermostat effect to start with and then the resulting target adjustment for 2012. I still see the reaction of my staff in my mind's eye. ;-) I had the feeling that they were asking among themselves what I'd smoked.

After the initial reactions, I presented my ideas for implementation. The figures now became clearer: Which turnover had to be achieved in which departments and how it would work.

My team was still very critical, but also saw the opportunities. From then on, all the topics on the agenda were viewed with the "spectacles" of doubling turnover. A strong internal dynamic developed over those four days. I remember a situation in which

Lisa proposed a measure and I thought that it would be far too expensive. She then responded that we had to think in other budgets, too, if we wanted to achieve the 2012 targets. She was right! It was a steep learning curve for me as well!

"If we align ourselves with what we are and what we can do, we'll remain static. If we align ourselves with our goals, we'll grow!"

Beginning September 2011, we started off our daily business highly motivated. But it felt different. The whole team was somehow operating on auto-pilot. Destination: Doubling 2012!

First results: The second semester of 2011 was better than the first semester. That had never happened to us before! The first semester contains five and a half "season months". The second semester has only three and a half months in which we can invoice in full. We take into account the holiday period in particular. The result was even more impressive in the light of the fact that our business is a very long-term one. Wow!

So we ended off 2011 with 25% more than the annual target!

A few weeks later there was another meeting in Mallorca. Currently, we are 8% below target for our sales projections for 2012. Wow! All of us in the team walk around with wide grins on our faces. We're enjoying our success. But wait: Don't think all our actions were successful as well! Nope, we also gave a few projects a resounding "fail". But the direction was always right.

What am I trying to tell you? I think that if it worked for me and my ten employees, it will work for you as well! Have a look at where you are clinging to a certain "temperature", where you want to develop further in yourself or in your business. Set yourself new development targets and develop the right measures to implement. And then you convince your team, your customers and your surroundings.

If you want to benefit from my experience in this, I look forward to you coming to my seminar and presentation and/or using the corresponding further training media!

On "Falling" and "Getting Up Again" — Not Only in Sales

It is said that "falling" is not so bad, as long as you don't "stay down". But the guy who does the falling definitely regards it as a bad thing.

Many successful Hollywood movies make use of the template of the shattered person who later turns into a hero. We like these stories of falling and getting back up again in our real everyday lives, not only in fiction.

This pattern really caught my attention when I first attended the National Speakers' Congress in the USA. Almost every keynote there had poached this subject as its "red thread". Granted, the dose makes the poison: It got on my nerves. It creates the impression that a career in my industry only happens to Americans as a stroke of bad personal luck or upgrading from working in a scullery before.

In Germany the culture is different: We tend to be more cautious and skeptical about someone who's "down". An example? Our colleague Jürgen Höller. He was right at the top in New Economy times: Owner of a business that was valued at 500 million dollars on the stock market. At the same time, he filled large halls in Germany as a speaker. He was Number 1. With lots of space to spare.

Then he fell. Far. Including imprisonment and debts into the millions. But he didn't stay down.

I was one of the first colleagues to appear together with Jürgen Höller 2.0. It was fascinating how many people accosted me about this: "How can you work with this man?" Even more fascinating, however, is the fact that to this day not a single customer has criticized me for this cooperation. It was always only people in the industry who did! I enjoyed collaborating with him! It was successful, and I was able to learn a lot from Jürgen.

I knew Jürgen Höller 1.0 only from the press and from his books. Of course I weighed my options. I gathered information. Also from his book *Und immer wieder aufstehen!* [Always get up again!], which he wrote during his "time out" and in which he gives profound insights into his (spiritual) life. In the final analysis, there was only one decision for me and my conscience: You want to work with this man!

Falling and getting up again. Few people show their hands the way he has. Brave!

Therefore… What am I trying to tell you?

Firstly: If you fall — which I don't wish upon you — get up again quickly!

Secondly: You can learn more from those who have fallen and are successful today than from those who have always been successful.

Thirdly: As a salesperson, you can benefit from your customers' crises as well. He who stands in partnership with his customer in bad times will later often enjoy unbeatable customer loyalty.

In the fourth place: Be morally "in the clear" with your customers. (At this point I am reminded of the event manager of a well-known insurance company, who actually asked me if I was willing to work for the company at all, because it was currently not "discussed" positively in the press!)

The Law of Numbers

The ice hockey legend Wayne Gretzky was once asked how come he consistently scored more goals than any other player in the league. His reply was simple and astounding at the same time: "You must shoot at goal at every opportunity. I've shot at goal a hundred times more than any other player!"

That is the law of numbers!

I am convinced that diligence is a fundamental virtue in sales and acquisition! What's more important — apart from pure quantity — is the quality of the customer contact. At the right moment — with the right customer — correctly prepared — with the right offer! I call that "sales and acquisition intelligence". And that is what I think!

Performance From Passion — Born To Sell

The singer Jürgen Drews was in his car on his way to one of his appearances in the rural areas. After a long search, he found a bar. The guests were amazed. What was he doing there? Jürgen Drews said that he was doing a gig there that night. The barman explained to him that the place, date and time would have been correct, but that it was the wrong year. The performance was only for the following year! A misunderstanding.

The singer then went to his car, fetched his guitar and celebrated with the guests until late that night!

Change of location: The singer Pavarotti gave a concert in Austria. He and his team had rented a villa for the trip. After the concert, everybody cooked and ate together. After supper, Pavarotti and his team sang more of his favorite songs. Just to end off a good day on a high note.

Both of them do what they do out of passion. Both love singing and enjoying time with other people. That they also earn good money doing it, is incidental.

And us salespeople? It is often said that salespeople are very money-driven. And I think that that's OK! Money is a form of recognition and gives you the freedom to do what you like doing. Money is a good thing.

However, I will allege that someone who does something only for money will never achieve in his profession what would have been possible with passion!

Who wins the battle? An army of mercenaries who fight for money or an army of volunteers who fight for their ideals, values, their fatherland and freedom?

What do you fight for in sales?

Does your job end at a specific time on the clock? Are weekends off-limits? Or do you read newspapers with the ulterior motive of how you can exploit the information gained in a targeted manner in your everyday sales work? Do you maybe come across an interesting report on a potential new customer who you then phone the next day? Or do you read a fascinating article that you send on to one of your regular customers because you think they'll be happy about the news?

Open day at your customer on a weekend. Do you go? Do you maybe even take your family along? Are you proud to show them who you do business with?

A car next to you in a traffic jam, covered in advertising. Contact details included. A potential new customer for you? Do you Google them later? Do you call them?

I'm convinced that top performance can only be achieved with passion! Born to sell!

Happy New Acquisition Year!

A warm welcome to the new year!

... and? Do you have good resolutions for the new year? Or maybe even concrete goals?

I don't think I need to explain the importance of goals to you anymore. Somehow it's a trend topic at the moment and everyone is talking about it. Let's rather talk about a far more decisive success factor when setting goals: Writing them down!

In 2006 *USA Today* published a study in which researchers observed a representative group of people with their "good resolutions for the new year". After exactly twelve months, the researchers took stock and made an astonishing discovery: Only 4% of the participants kept their resolutions if they hadn't written them down! In contrast, 44% of those of those who wrote down their thoughts kept their resolutions!

That does not mean that clear and written goals are a guarantee for more success in life/and/or sales, but the probability of success increases tenfold!

Writing is a "psychoneuromotor" activity. Writing forces us to think about things and to concentrate better. Writing down our own goals ensures that we have to decide what we want, what our priorities in life are.

"You either work at realizing your own goals, or you work at enriching other people's goals!" ... says my American colleague Brian Tracy.

For me personally, the "Goal-setting ritual" has become more and more refined every year: I always document my financial and entrepreneurial goals with my closest employees during a summer break on Mallorca, and again at the turn of the year for myself. I always set my personal goals around the time of my birthday in September. For me it works to do this in stages. In this way, I remove the complexity for myself.

Reinhold Würth says: "Our core competence is marketing and selling. There are other people who can also do fastening technology." Reinhold Würth is a salesperson — through and through — and the success of his business can clearly be traced back to good sales and selling work. What is your core competence? On the next pages you'll get concrete ideas for increasing your customer numbers and transactions. Have fun!

Is it Possible To "Polish Through" a Windscreen? Extreme Sales Volumes at Red Traffic Lights

I wonder: Is it possible to "polish through" a windscreen? In the last half hour, the windscreen of my rented car has been wiped four times already by some adolescent at a red traffic light. This is how it is here in the Caribbean. You can buy fruit, telephone cards, chargers, wiper blades, drinks and much more at every traffic light. The street sellers besiege the cars.

I am particularly popular here: When I rent a car here, I always choose an affordable small car, as inconspicuous as possible and with many miles on the clock. Yet the street sellers here have special eyes. A few hundred yards away they know: Here comes a potential customer, a tourist! At the latest when they can see

I'm the driver, it's clear to them: This one has potential! I just look very different to the locals.

I can glare at them, wave them off with a casual hand signal, protest loudly, or just not react at all. None of it is any use. He has potential, he will be canvassed. Whether I want to or not!

The young boy throws his wet sponge onto my windscreen from five yards away. Then he approaches and wipes everything thoroughly. When... there is nothing to wipe! His three colleagues already did the whole job before him.

And? Well, yes, I give him some money. It's called the "debt of gratitude" or the "principle of reciprocity". He was polite. He made an effort. He has nothing else. My good deed for today. But I've done enough good deeds for a month today.

What can we as salespeople learn from these experiences?

1. To have or develop an eye for potential!

2. Whether they want to or not: just talk to them first. And then see how the situation develops. How many sales deals or appointments have I seen where the customers had previously rejected a decision to buy with all their might!? How many conversations have I had in which the customer objected right at the beginning that they didn't have time, but that I had to end?

3. The debt of gratitude works very well with us, too. Business is done between people, after all. Find a good solution for using this behavior pattern with your customers as well.

Deutsche Bahn And "Selling"? Find the Mistake.

Recently at the Deutsche Bahn ticket counter at Frankfurt airport:

"To Bochum main station, please! The quickest possible way!"

"You can take the train at 07:10 a.m. just now and you'll be in Bochum in less than two hours."

And then: "Would you like a ticket for first class, which is more comfortable, and for even better service?"

A real advantage argument. Friendly! Professional. Wow! Yes, I know, those in the know would say that it would have been even better if the benefit for the customer had been emphasized even more: "so that you're even more relaxed when you arrive" or "so that you can enjoy a tasty breakfast served conveniently right at your seat..." etc.

Apart from the impressive advantage argument, the man at the counter also made an up-sell: the expensive first-class ticket instead of the standard ticket. The benefit for the railways: more revenue. The benefit to me: see above.

"Would you like to be sure and reserve your seat as well?" Welcome to cross-selling: selling a useful complementary product or service. Well done!

"Can that still be done at such short notice?" — my buying signal!

A sales conversation in 30 seconds! With advantage arguments and additional sales by up-selling and cross-selling. And this at Deutsche Bahn. I am impressed.

What I missed: Why didn't he offer me a railways card? I wasn't impatient at the time, nor was there a long queue of other customers waiting behind me. It would definitely have been appropriate.

And what can you take from this for your business?

1. The sales wording in the customer advantage argument.

2. Up-selling: Provide better quality, a larger quantity, a longer duration — for the "good" of your customer.

3. Cross-selling: Always offer the right additional performance: Products and services.

4. Be even more aggressive with the additional offers if the customer does not stop you themselves.

The incredible revenue potential lies in the supplementary sales! Many businesses live only off supplementary sales!

Lufthansa Does Away with First Class on Many Routes — a Disaster of Sales Psychology!

This can only be the idea of an accountant who makes decisions based on numbers: The luxury class at Lufthansa is canceled! Of courses costs can be saved in the short term if you do this, but in the long term it's an own goal for the company.

In sales psychology, we align ourselves with reference values: Imagine that you want to buy a holiday home on Mallorca. You imagine a price of around one million dollars. Now the property broker shows you three properties in one day: First, a villa of three million dollars. You like it, but it's outside of your budget planning. Then the house in need of renovation in the second row for $850,000. That's not for you. Out of the question. Then, lastly, the elegant house for 1.25 million dollars. Even if it doesn't quite compare with the villa from the first viewing appointment, you like it. And your budget? You are happy to extend it because you've seen what else you'll get for your money on *Mallorca*. Conclusion: You are basing your decision on the reference values of the first two houses!

Car manufacturers use the same psychological effect: Volkswagen has the Phaeton, Mercedes has the Maybach. All of this just so that you haven't reached the end of the price flagpole with the S-class. The result:

TIP

Even if the premium products themselves are not the best sellers, they make it much easier to raise the average price.

One of my customers, one of the best fitness clubs in Germany, offered two types of memberships: For $50 and for $80. Most of the memberships were in the $50 class. No wonder: There was no premium value. After a third variant was offered for $120 and it was also only first mentioned in the consultation, sales of the $80 membership increased drastically!

If Lufthansa now cancels their First Class, Business Class suddenly becomes the most expensive variant and will encourage the accountant to activate cost-cutting measures on the customer side and encourage business travelers to fly economy in future. The consequence is an own goal with regards to the average price of all tickets.

That's what happens when management accountants take over marketing.

Examples: Manuel Neuer, Cristiano Ronaldo and Tom Peters

The European Football Championship left its mark even in my family: During a game in the garden, my six-year-old son suddenly isn't called Ben anymore, but rather Manuel Neuer. He comments on every goalkeeper save as if he were the goalkeeper of the national team. I regard it as special recognition that he now calls my shots at goal Cristiano Ronaldo.

Role models are especially important for children's development. I'm not telling parents anything new here.

My first professional role model as trainer and speaker was the American management guru Tom Peters. Of course I'm familiar with all his books, all videos and his PowerPoint presentations which he very generously makes available on the Internet. I read what he says on Twitter daily. He's been my benchmark for almost 20 years.

For me he was the first one to not only write good books, but also to present these books graphically in such a way that it's fun to read them again and again. For me, the best one is still *Circle of Innovation*, published in 1997. But not only did Peters write brilliant books, a book was even written about him: 1998 *The Tom Peters Phenomenon — The Rise of a Management Guru* by Stuart Crainer. A reading tip for all (prospective) speakers.

Why is he specifically such a special person to me? Apart from his ideas, stimuli, his expertise: He is incredibly inquisitive! He wants his gravestone to read: "He was curious to the end!" Peters reads a book (ONE BOOK!!) per day. He has an incredible competitive advantage: He needs only three to four hours sleep per night! I, myself, am impressed by his mixture of extremely extroverted presentation before large masses of people and his contrast program: He lives in a rural area two hours removed from the nearest large airport and there he writes his books and articles in retreat.

That impresses me. That is a lifestyle I like. Now, as for the few hours of sleep per night, I'd only last one night, but the rest...

But the Competition Is Not the Challenge! The Customer Is!

A few days ago I returned from Dallas with my closest staff members. Five days of further training at the largest trainers' congress: the ASTD Convention (American Society of Training and Development) with more than 9,000 participants from all over the world.

In addition to many interesting impressions on the topic of training, a figure from the subject of "Sales" impressed me in particular:

58% don't make a decision!

According to a study, 58% of customers DO NOT MAKE a purchasing decision! And here most salespeople think that the competitor is the real challenge when it comes to generating revenue! Wrong! If the customer is not completely convinced, no time "pressure" is built up or the purchasing decision is not a priority, the customer just DOES NOT make a decision.

The bad part: You don't make any turnover. The good part: The competitor also doesn't. And in most cases, the customer's concrete need remains in place. Well, hope floats…

Now that means: All of us lose orders, not to better products, better services or better prices. We lose orders to better salespeople: to salespeople that don't only advise, but also motivate the customer to make a decision to buy! Now! Or at the latest at follow-up!

And what is the "recipe" for "motivating customers to make a purchasing decision"? Well, for a recipe the first thing you need are the ingredients. These are: best preparation, appointment, appointment confirmation with contents, creating a relationship level, optimal determination of needs and requirements, motive to buy, moral preliminary contract, argumentation of advantages with customer success stories, open opinion questions, recognizing buying signals, concluding at the right time, securing with a confirmation of purchase.

Okay. The ingredients are right. Now it depends on doing it in the right order and in the correct dosage. But that is beyond the scope of this text.

How Can Salespeople Learn from People Who Deliver Parcels? The Law of Numbers.

DHL parcel deliverers deliver 85 parcels each a day, as I found out last week. Wow! 85 every day! Regardless of whether the traffic or weather plays along.

In sales terms, the number 85 here stands for the "hit rate". And in sales, "success" is composed of "hit rate" (quantity) and "impact" (quality):

H + H = S

Let's relate the number of the parcel deliverers to that of a telephone salesperson: My telesales employees in the team make a hit rate of 80 gross calls (call attempts) outbound when they address business customers on corporate seminars.

100 when it's about tickets for our events (*Bestseller Forum, Sales Offensive*...). The difference is in the length of the conversation. Here too, it means: Every day! No difference, whether it's Monday or Friday.

The 75 telesales employees of one of my customers who sells a product with a short sales cycle to business customers also make 100 a day.

For call center agents with inbound calls (the customer calls in) the number is significantly higher: depending on customer group and product I know about numbers between 180 and 300.

The hit rates in the field vary a lot! That is very individual.

**H + H = S is the so-called "law of numbers".
Or to put it differently: the more contacts,
the more contracts.**

Conclusion: Apart from your selling skill (impact), how high is your hit rate? How diligent are you? Or your team?

Can you name your hit rate? Have you ever measured your hit rate over a longer period of time? Have you ever analyzed your hit rate in relation to your orders (success)?

Hmmm... maybe you think that you're also that successful. If so, well, "congratulations"! Yet... have you ever considered how successful you could be if you increased the hit rate (with at least the same impact) even more?

What do you think? Should a salesperson who did good turnover in the morning reduce their hit rate for the rest of the day? Or is it a matter of the piece of sales wisdom: When the going is good, you should do more?

I know many salespeople who are satisfied with their results, who have settled down in their comfort zone and are therefore lagging behind in their sales potential.

The "Cleaning Lady Call" — a Pricing Tactic

A while ago I was in a large furniture store with my son Ben. Shopping without time pressure for a change. Ben was just testing the slide of a children's bunk bed and indicated to me that this could still take some time. So I could observe consultations from afar: An extended Turkish family was having a corner sofa presented to them by a salesperson. The purchase decision was taken quite quickly… But there were still some questions to be clarified. The salesperson went around the corner to his desk about 16 yards away, not visible to the customer. He sat down and did nothing. Nothing at all! About three or four minutes passed — so around ten quick slide tests by Ben — until he got up again and went back to the customer group. I couldn't hear anything, they were all too far away, but I knew exactly what the topic was right then: The salesperson shook his head and put on a disappointed face. Welcome to the price conversation!

To the customer's question about a discount, the salesperson reacted with "I'll have to ask" or "I'll look in the computer if there are any possibilities". But that was only a pretext. For him it was about gaining time and giving the customer the impression that he negotiated "hard". All tactics!

When the customer had signed the purchase contract, Ben had also finished his test series.

As coincidence would have it, a few days ago the sales manager of a Vienna furniture chain came to one of my presentations. I told him about my experience. We were both grinning. He revealed to me: That is a "cleaning lady call" ;-)

Conclusion: There are countless tactics you can use in a sales negotiation! You should know all of them, because especially professional shoppers like to use them to their advantage. You need "equality of arms". Do you know, for example, the difference between "I'll look in the computer" or "I'll do some calculations again to see if we can do something…" and "I'm going to consult someone" or "I have to ask my boss" (or the "cleaning lady call")?

If you yourself "do some calculations again", you signal to the customers that you are competent in questions of price as well. You remain on equal terms.

If you use the "ask the boss" variant, you commit price competence suicide. You signal that you can advise well, but only up to the question of the price. Now the customer learns: in case of discounts, always talk to the boss about it!

**Even if you have to talk to the boss, always choose the wording which gives the impression that you can decide everything yourself.
No one has to hear that call ;-)**

The master thesis — or:
Know in Advance Where the Potential Is

A company from northern Germany wanted to expand into the Eastern European market with its products, electronically controlled pig feeding systems. The east is particularly interesting because there are very large pig farms. Yet where specifically should the sales department start with the acquisition? Where exactly are the potential customers?

The company hired a few interns for a few weeks to help develop an appropriate acquisition strategy. Students who were native to the target countries and had a perfect command of the language. They first researched the internet and authorities to determine where the large feedlots are located. Then they called them, determined the relevant contact person and started with a telephone interview: They were students writing their master thesis in Germany and had a few questions: "How many animals? What type of feed? How is it fed: in solid or liquid form? How old is the feeding system? Any planned investments?" The person called usually gave information willingly, because they felt flattered that a student took the trouble to call them from far away Germany.

After a few weeks, the sales department knew exactly which customers were worthwhile and which farms would only be contacted later or not at all. A brilliant strategy!

Note: Yes, the interns were students. I do not know what they were studying. I will never know whether they wrote a master thesis about this or another subject. Now: Everything you say must be true. But you don't have to say everything that is true.

Authority Is Derived from the Author…
and If I Have Nothing to Say?
Then You Can Show Something

As a book author, you are already someone "special" in Germany. And you can also reach new customers very well with a textbook, of course. Knowledge workers, such as consultants, trainers and speakers, absolutely need a book to document their expertise: Authority is derived from the author! But what can you do if you have too little "knowledge" to produce a meaningful textbook? Why not publish an illustrated book? Show instead of tell!

Surely you ask yourself now: "With an illustrated book? What's that supposed to mean?"

A case study: The market leader for natural stones, such as marble or granite for floors, bathrooms and kitchens, has published a very beautiful illustrated book: The journey of the stone from the quarry in Brazil or Italy, through the huge warehouse in Germany, to the stonemason and the destination point at the customer's buildings. Everything is documented with magnificent photos.

These photos are from customer projects of the stonemasons. Both the product and the workmanship of the craftsmen are presented here in an ideal form.

The illustrated book achieves two objectives: The importer ties the customers permanently to his business, and, at the same time, the stonemason can use the book actively during the consultation, showing the customer what is possible. Moreover, the book is a special proof of competence: the high-quality illustrated book, which the craftsman then usually gives to the customer as a personal gift.

Convincing Through Witnesses: Customer Events to Acquire New Customers

The target group of a company from a suburb in Bochum (Dortmund) are property managers who sell metrology. Every year in September, the company organizes an exciting customer event.

In the morning, the invited guests enjoy interesting presentations by external speakers on the hottest specialist topics in an exclusive hotel. After an extended lunch, follow the presentations of the internal experts. A day filled with know-how in a special ambiance. The participants are enthusiastic and also receive an indirect purchase confirmation as customers: This is the right partner for my business!

A successful event. But where is the acquisition of new customers supposed to be here?

Most companies use such events only for customer retention because they only invite their existing top customers. The company from Dortmund follows another strategy. Only 30 to 50% of their existing customers are invited. 50 to 70% of the guests are potential new customers, who have not yet bought from the company. The seating arrangement for the morning presentations is fixed: The place cards are based on the following system: new customer — existing customer — new customer — existing customer. At the large, round tables, every guest has another seat neighbor during lunch, yet the system remains in place. Also in the afternoon new table neighbors determine the picture of the presentations with the same system. Officially, this procedure is justified with "promoting the exchange between colleagues" — in more modern terms: Networking. But psychologically, there is even more to it: In an ideal scenario, a new customer met six enthusiastic existing customers as seat neighbors during the event day. What did they talk about? About the excellent company and the exclusive event, of course. Naturally, the existing customer has been to several of these events and raves about the company. What do the "not yet buying" guests take home from it?

The sales employees for metrology are there as well, of course. But they are not allowed to actively canvass on this day! Guests are supposed to have an extraordinary nice day and, if at all, approach the salesperson with business subjects only on their own accord.

Two to three days after the event, the salespeople become active. Every guest and also every potential new customer is being contacted telephonically. In doing so, the salespeople follow a certain pattern:

1. "Thank you for attending!"

2. "How did you like the event?"

3. "What was the most important information you got from the presentations?"

4. "May we invite you again next year?" These four steps are a type of debt of gratitude to the conversation partner. The expert term is: Reciprocity principle. All this is only the purposeful preparation to get to the actual goal.

5. "If you enjoyed the event this much and already got the first impression of our company, how interesting would it be for you if we sat together again and looked at the advantages you would have from working with us?"

The appointment rate is close to the 100% mark. Morally, the customer can hardly decline the request for an appointment. And the salesperson does not really have to sell. The existing customers have already done all the convincing during the event. Convincing through witnesses!

Variants of this method: You do not have your own customer event? Then get involved in another event. Regional marketing clubs offer a club evening once a month. In most cases, interesting speakers have been booked for a talk. For a fee, you can participate, even if you are not a member, and you can bring guests.

A few years ago, the marketing club in my neighboring city invited me to a talk in the soccer stadium "Arena auf Schalke." A tour of the stadium and a marketing presentation to advertise the location. As well as tasty catering and plenty of space for networking. I spontaneously invited a few soccer-mad customers and asked them to please bring along friends and business partners.

One customer traveled for two hours to get there and brought two business partners with him simultaneously. What do you think they spoke about on the way home? Well, after the presentation and over a glass of beer, the business partners asked me if I could also accompany this and that task in their companies. Buying signals! I also did not have to canvass actively in this situation. My customer had already done the selling on the way to the event.

Mailings and Telephone Acquisition? And If They Are Not Suitable?

An experienced attorney leaves a company and opens his own law firm. His field of expertise: What legalities do Swiss companies have to consider when working with German companies. And vice versa. His advantage: He is admitted to the bar in Switzerland as well as in Germany. Now it is all about attracting new clients. And he starts off his client list at zero. In our view, the classic acquisition methods such as mailings and cold calling are not suitable for this particular topic. Therefore, our first advice for the attorney in this situation was: Piggyback marketing.

He offers the southern German Chamber of Commerce and Industry a day or evening seminar on this topic. In this way, he gets close to the participants and will usually be approached directly by possible clients. Because the seminar is held rather superficially. Details are always company-specific. And just like that, he is in a canvassing appointment. A nice side effect: Apart from his fee and travel expenses, he also receives up to six months of advertising opportunities because he appears in the calendar of events of the Chamber.

Another channel for acquisition are the fireplace evenings of many Swiss trustees who want to offer their best clients something special in the fourth quarter of the year: Wealthy top clients are invited to a stylish dinner. Afterward, the attorney gives a witty speech on his topic. No more than three-quarters of an hour and laced with anecdotes. After that, high-level networking starts around the fireplace. Here he also receives a recognition fee, and his expenses are paid for, apart from interesting business cards.

A Car Pool as an Acquisition Tool

In agriculture, farmers are always invited by the agricultural trade and industry to see the effects of products for themselves. For this purpose, for example, the so-called "Field Day" is organized. A manufacturer of crop protection products presents the application results on a corn field. Of course, the guests' culinary needs are also being taken care of. The regionally responsible sales representative of the respective agricultural product dealer organizes car pools for his clients. The farmers usually know each other well. The car pools are put together according to the following pattern: Two existing customers drive together with a potential new customer in one car — one hour there, one hour back. What are they talking about while driving? Who does the convincing?

Thanks to the prior piggyback marketing, the salesperson basically only has to collect the order in the following week.

Trojan Mailing

The success of a mailing is usually regarded as being due to good addresses or an interesting layout of the paper message. But there are other ways that lead to success: A few years ago, I was supposed to market the predecessor of the *Bestseller Forum*. A presentation program of the best speakers in the areas of distribution, marketing and sales. The interested target group for this event is responsible parties in marketing, sales, and management. These people are organized, for example, in the marketing club. So, I started a cooperation with a regional marketing club: At the time, the club was still inviting 1,500 members by letter to its events each month. By me taking over postage and packaging, the club was willing to enclose the event brochure to the club letter and also to point out the special conditions for members in the P.S. The result was an incredible response rate!

These days, promotional letters with unknown senders usually land straight in the paper recycling bin. The receiver trusts the marketing club as a sender and is interested in opening the letter. Therefore, ask yourself:

TIP

Who does your target group trust? Who walks in and out of there? And who could deliver your advertising message that way?

20 to 30% More Turnover on Almost Every Order — Certainly!

At the time, I was prepared to spend $599 for my first iPad. However, it turned out to be more than $1,000. And I had a really good feeling about it. Why?

"I would like to get the smallest and cheapest iPad," I explained to the salesperson at Gravis. — "What would you like to do with it?" he asked (= needs and situation analysis — what does the customer really need?). — "It is for my two children. So they do not get bored during long car rides," — "and how many movies should be on the device?" was his question. — "20? There should be some kind of a selection to choose from."

And just like that, we arrived at the device with the largest storage space. Oh yes, and at the most expensive one! (= upselling — to sell a larger quantity or a better quality of a product).

Afterward, I also purchased the earphone adaptor because both children were supposed to see and listen at the same time after all. $16.00. Then the adaptor for the memory card and the usb stick: $32.00. And the neoprene case to protect the iPad: $29.00. And… and… and… (= cross-selling — to sell products that complement each other).

After 15 minutes I left the shop with great new products and a credit card slip for over $1,000. And I was feeling great, too. I had found the perfect product solution for my action plan.

Every additional option made sense to me. During the months following the purchase, it turned out that the salesperson had done a perfect job. Perfect for me as a user. But also perfect for the turnover of his employer.

If you as a salesperson know how to do it, then achieving 20 to 30% more turnover is child's play.

"Is This Real?" … or How You Receive Maximum Attention

Is this real?

Mail: A birthday card from Miles & More. An A5 card was fully written. Written? In beautiful calligraphy and blue ink, the sender writes to me about all the nice things he wishes for me.

Half of the office discusses with me whether this is a special printing technique or whether an actual human wrote these five sentences with care and effort by hand.

Because I am so impressed and at the same time curious, we continue the discussion via Facebook and Co. There is the suggestion to wet my thumb and test whether the ink is real. And … it is! Wow!

TIP

Whatever the sender's intention was by writing the card: Now a few thousand people know about it! Maximum attention!

And this even though I am critical of the effectiveness of mailings.

In this context, I have learned that with the SCHREIBSTATT (www.schreibstatt.de), we can also attract this extraordinary attention from our customers and business partners. At this provider, already more than fifty calligraphers write up to three thousand birthday cards, package inserts, addresses on envelopes, and anything else the heart desires. Each copy is an original, so it will easily withstand my print analysis.

Conclusion: If you want to stand out from the crowd with your mailing, it has to be *positively unusual*.

If You Do Not Follow Up, You Insult the Customer!

Thursday evening. Dinner with friends. The topic of the conversation: Experiences with craftsmen. One in our circle just bought a house and tells us about his experiences with craftsmen. A lot of positive things. But also thrilling anecdotes from the field, *no one will believe that*! For example, he asked for quotations for an 80,000 dollar pool. The thrilling aspect: None of the providers asks what he would like to do now. No one follows up! It is a good reason to shake their heads for the salespeople around the table. For us it is incomprehensible: A craftman has put a lot of effort, time, and know-how into creating the offer, and now he is waiting for THE CUSTOMER to get back to him ...

This is where two different philosophies meet: The customer is disappointed, that the craftsman does not get back to him, in fact, shows his lack of interest, indirectly insults him, signals to him: Accept it or leave it! And the craftsman is disappointed in the customer: He has already invested a lot in taking the measurements and creating the offer, and then the customer does not even get back to him! Outrageous!

Here we need a clarification of the roles:

A call to everyone who sends out quotations: Do follow up! Rather late than never. Follow up until you get the order or until the order has been placed with someone else. This can also mean that you follow up again and again on your quotation for up to two years! Do not give up!

Men can compare this situation to social canvassing: After the first meeting, telephone numbers are exchanged, and then HE is annoyed because SHE does not make contact? Find the mistake.

In honor of all the craftsmen, I was able to share my experiences with car dealers that evening when I wanted to purchase two new premium leasing vehicles for my employees a few years ago, in the middle of the recession. Again, no one followed up.

Conclusion: It was a really nice evening... and you can be remembered in a positive light if you follow up diligently on your quotations in the future.

What Is Better? Knife, Fork, Spoon, or New Customer Acquisition?

What is better? Knife, fork, or spoon? You cannot say that? Why? Oh... it depends on what you want to eat? Absolutely... A knife and a bowl of soup are not really compatible.

This is instantly obvious when it comes to cutlery. The goal determines the tool. But when it comes to sales, this is not so obvious for most people. Some myths persist.

Every quarter I follow the Xenagos-Sales-Indicator with great interest. In a special query, I was asked for an additional answer: "If you look at a normal week or a normal month, what percentage of your sales activity is attributed to new customer business?"

Independent of the result of this survey: What are the answers supposed to tell us? Do you want to use the figures as benchmarks for yourself and your team? Have a look at how much energy other salespeople invest in the subject of acquisition?

This will rarely ever match. Because: The goals determine the tools.

TIP

Reduced to the essentials: Company goals determine the sales goals. These in turn determine the measures and the necessary tools. And not new customer acquisition because others do it or because it just fits into the sales management's action plan.

What are your goals? What is your strategy?

An estate agent for villas in Mallorca, a property developer with townhouses for young families, a company that sells prefabricated houses… Yes, they will generate their growth almost exclusively through new customers. Here the sales strategy of acquisition fits.

Acquisition for a wholesaler with several thousand contacts in his customer list, on the other hand, is usually the wrong path. Here growth comes from extracting potential from his existing customers. Upselling and optimization of order volumes or cross-selling. Even if the salespeople would not acquire one single new customer for a year, a good growth spurt could still be achieved.

Conclusion: Your goals determine your measures — not only in sales!

"10 + 1 = 10" or: Why Wanting More Does Not Automatically Mean Having More

Many centuries ago, the first diamond was discovered. It was said then that the light lives within it. And of course, a diamond meant immeasurable wealth. When a farmer in far-away India heard about it, he went to search for this diamond. He searched for years and everywhere in this world. He risked all his possession and, in the end, lost everything he owned during his search. He died somewhere in Europe. Poor and without ever having found a diamond. A few years later, diamonds were found on the former property of the farmer. So many diamonds, that the place of discovery was turned into one of the biggest diamond mines in the world.

And the moral of the story…

The winner of the Bestseller Awards 2014, the company Würth, has a very specific sales formula: 10 + 1 = 10. You may ask now how the company could become so successful, even though they do not know their math? Yet the formula does not represent a mathematic equation but rather that *wanting more* not automatically means *having more.*

Salespeople always want an even broader range of product options and product versions. Salespeople always want even more customers, more target groups, and a larger area. But this is often a fallacy: Existing range (10) plus new products (1) does not always equal more turnover (10/11). The same goes for the size of the area.

The most limiting factor is time: Every salesperson has only 24 hours in a day. This time cannot be multiplied. And it is also the limiting factor on the side of the customer: Customers have a limited attention span. They are not prepared to listen to endless presentations.

TIP

Conclusion: Instead of constantly striving for even more, it makes more sense and is more profitable to get the maximum out of your area, out of the existing range. Focus on what is there and utilize your potential.

Würth goes even further: Growth through cell division. Once a salesperson has built up an area in a period of about three years, the company divides the region into three parts. In a period of two to three years, the salesperson then has the task of raising the former turnover again to the same level. The salespeople do not find this approach funny. But the success proves the company right.

Frank's Got It! … And How Do You Make Your Customers Even More Successful?

Frank is my insurance broker. But this is not all: We are friends, exercise together, and share a lot of business ideas. Insurance sales is a people business. Relationship sales.

In particular, the salesperson's personality makes the difference with products such as insurances or financial services. Frank is mastering this with me in an exemplary manner. But also with his other customers: He organizes a regular's table for his existing and new customers: A guest speaker gives a few impulses to the group and then the exchange continues during dinner. In modern terms: Networking.

One thing I naturally find even more interesting: He invites interested parties and customers to my sales offense in Bochum twice a year. He organizes the car pools, tickets, seating reservations, lunches, and the talk with the speaker. He actually helps his customers to become even more successful in their own businesses! Do I have to mention that his company rates are among the best in financial terms?

And what do you do to stand out from the competition? What do you do to make your customers even more successful?

The invitation to a NASCAR race or a major league soccer final is very cool, but it holds no business sustainability. Furthermore, corporate compliance policies are increasingly stringent. One of my customers has two business boxes in a major league soccer stadium. But many invitations to come there are being declined! The risk that the TV cameras zoom in and result in "funny" situations afterward is too great.

Ah … once again Frank. He often gives his customers specialist books that he himself recommends and has read. Very individual, very budget-friendly, and yet with a strong effect because he signals to his customer that he is thinking of him and has thought about his daily business. Of course, I also like it.

Conclusion: Inspire your customers, seek personal contact, offer added value. If you do not have any other ideas, you have to differentiate through your price structure and lose orders to better salespeople!

It Feels As If You Have Become a Dad — Customers Do Not Buy Products but the Story That Comes With Them.

Some idle time during a hotel breakfast. Time to read the small print on the packet of teabags: Product: Earl Grey tea. Sales approach: Convincing through witnesses. "The manufacturer of this tea already supplied the second Earl Grey," is the reference the sixth Earl Grey gives. Message: Tradition, experience. It has to be good. And then, a brief history of the company follows. Conclusion: Well done! Now I am drinking not just any black tea but a part of British tradition. Already tastes different.

It is similar with Red Bull: The founder of the company, Dietrich Mateschitz, already mentioned more than ten years ago during an interview that initially, it was not allowed to sell Red Bull in Germany. Some ingredients were not compatible with the Food Act. In retrospect, this was a blessing for the product. The Bavarians *smuggled* it from Austria and thus created a myth. When the drink was finally legalized, the feeling that it was something illegal, something exceptional, remained. And this was priceless marketing. Red Bull is not only by far the market leader but has also invented its own market. This myth also ensures that the competition is kept at bay.

14 years ago, I bought a so-called lemon car which caused me a lot of hassles. I was looking for a 100 % reliable car, and Mercedes claimed at that time that they were building the best car: the S-class. The dealer recommended that I collect it straight from the factory. I traveled in the morning. Premium reception. Lounge. Second breakfast. A movie about the history of Mercedes in the company's cinema. Followed by a factory tour. A detailed presentation of the production of the S-class hood. Crazy! Pure brainwashing! After more than two hours, I waited in the lounge for my car. From a height of 33 feet, one had a view into the hall where the cars were handed over to their proud owners with detailed instructions. Every two minutes, a gate opened, and a new vehicle was driven inside. What an arc of suspense! To me, it was almost compatible with the situation of becoming a father.

There is a paper factory in Gmund at the Tegernsee. A family business for many generations. Qualitatively in its own league. Here, customers quickly come to compare the product. But with what? It always ends in an apple-with-pears-comparison. Now the salespeople are called upon: The factory tour is one of the most powerful (sales and persuasion) tools. This is developed into a real experience. Anyone who has experienced this as a customer sees the product and its price-performance ratio completely differently.

Conclusion: We, as customers, do not just buy a product. We buy the story behind it.

Do you have such a story? Regarding your company, your products and/or a specific person in your company? With this approach, you create a clear differentiation from your competitors and anchor your message much better and more sustainably in your customer's mind.
So: Sell your story!

"Watch Out! She Is a Double-D!"

No, this is not what you think. No lingerie. Switch off the movie in your head. When I get a tip like that from one of my employees, I know I have to expect a very direct conversation partner when contacting the client. One who gets straight to the point and wants to have quick answers and results.

Many of our clients are *classified* by one or two letters. D, I, S, G — every letter stands for a preferred approach. For how someone feels particularly comfortable in a communication. If we know that, we will gladly adapt our communication accordingly. The conversations simply run more smoothly.

This helps with customer contact, with the acquisition. But most certainly does it help with the daily cooperation within the team. We are in a better position to gauge each other. That way, work runs more smoothly, too.

DISG is a scientifically based and, at the same time, very pragmatic tool that helps me to communicate better with other people. I have been working with it successfully since 1997.

You too can use the tips of the DISG model for even more successful conversations.

Sales Are Not Just a Department, but It Is All of Us in the Company — the SalesBattle

I love selling. So does my team. Every now and then, we have a SalesBattle: a day on which we let our daily business be and all employees make the telephone lines run hot by phoning the whole day. No e-mails, no quotations, no service calls. Only hit rate times impact. Follow-up sales with existing customers, activation of dormant customers, follow-up on quotations, phone around for follow-up, and naturally, cold calling. Only activities that lead to turnover.

Who wants to join? Everyone: from boss to trainee. With a tally chart on the whiteboard: Who sold what? And only this day counts. Everything that comes in afterward is appreciated but does not count into the contest.

My tip: This is also worth it for you and your team! Motivation and turnover. And the message is clear:

Sales is not just a department, but it is all of us in the company.

As a salesperson: Why not organize such a day with a few colleagues?

As the boss: Turn a day like this into a ritual. And participate in it as well. Of course, it would be great if you could also write some results on the whiteboard. But this is not the primary objective of this exercise.

Oh yes. I used to think there are only four *mortal enemies* of the salesperson: Spring, summer, fall, and winter! For a while now I have known that it is in actual fact five: Monday, Tuesday, Wednesday, Thursday, and Friday ;-) Forget all the beliefs about the summer slump! Sales ALWAYS works! So: Let's get started!

And: The result of a study which I just found on Twitter, fits in with this. Advertising emails have the best opening rates with potential new customers on Saturdays and Sundays! Who would have known? If we transfer this to *sales during the summer months*, unexpected opportunities arise.

"I Used to Be Like You"

I read an interesting story about Jung von Matt, one of Germany's most successful advertising agencies. They create the advertising, for example, Mercedes, Sixt or Bild.

The advertisers had the idea of supporting panhandlers: They wanted to improve the hand-written texts on the donation boxes. Because if corporations invest many thousands of dollars for this service, then the text from the pen of a professional will certainly increase the turnover of panhandlers.

Jung von Matt contacted the Berlin homeless magazine *Stuetze* and arranged (what was not so easy) a presentation appointment. The reactions of the Berlin panhandlers sounded familiar to the advertising pros:

"Nah, I've found my look."

"I don't want to change anything about my appearance. It could alienate my regulars."

"I think the texts are funny but it will certainly not work for the people."

"I don't want to decide straight away. I have to speak to a few pals first."

Do you also recognize these statements? Classic excuses and objections like you hear from customers in many sales talks and presentations. It does not matter if advertisers are pitching for a million-dollar budget or free signs for panhandlers. Skeptical people, fear of humor, fear of change, and the belief in one's own *market research*. Anyone who sells experiences these *standard situations*.

**So: Be well prepared for your standard situations in your response to excuses and objections.
A quick, rhetorical wit is not innate but trained.**

Some of the panhandlers could be convinced and they used signs with lines like: "I struggle with impermanence, but I accept small change. "Every throw a dollar," "I invested in Telekom shares," "T(r)ip me away from here," and "I used to be like you."

The result: The panhandlers who were active in their market with the new signs were able to increase their turnover by 25 to 30%, as was confirmed by the people from *Stuetze*.

It is wonderful if the bravery of trying something new is being rewarded instantly. And? What "new" things will you try in your new customer acquisition?

"Winning Interesting Customers from the Competition" ...

... was the biggest sales challenge in 2012, accounting for 44% of all mentions. according to 500 sales representatives from all industries surveyed as part of the DVKS annual survey.

If you want to market an innovation that enters a completely new market, then acquire entirely new customers. But that is the exception. As a matter of rule, the markets are fragmented, and you can be successful only by displacement, i.e., by attracting customers from the competition.

Competitive acquisition means that in preparation, you identify your target group precisely, find out which competitor is currently serving this target group, and then think about a strategy of how you will poach the customer.

When is the right time for that? For example, you can contact the customer by phone before an industry trade show and use the show as an excuse to get talking.

Which acquisition channel is the best? Telephone contact, mailing, trade shows etc.

How do you make your case? Pricing propositions? Service advantages? Or do you first unsettle the customer through intellectual arson ("Geistige Brandstiftung®")?

The first two points are often noted, but the actual argument is almost always developed after the process is already underway. And then it is often only a shoot from the hip.

TIP

In any case, you should have a good initial statement and then, of course, be prepared for your conversation partner's most important excuses and objections.

You will notice: There are always the same counterarguments. Thus, preparing for these standard answers is not a big challenge.

So what are the legal implications? Are you actually allowed to do that?

In a decision dated 1 March 2012, the Higher Regional Court Munich confirmed: Poaching of customers is often permissible in competition law.

Guideline: In principle, the enticing away of customers is only deemed unfair if special circumstances arise because, from the point of view of competition law, there is no entitlement to the continuation of the customer base.

So… what are you waiting for?

A Good Salesperson Determines the Pictures in the Head of His Customer — Magic Words for Marketing and Selling

I like salted butter. Not just any, but the French Président sea salt butter. Why? Because it is really tasty and on the other hand, because the story around the product inspires me.

Do you know that feeling when you have breakfast alone and then, more out of boredom than interest, read through the texts on the food packaging? That's what happened to me with Président butter.

"Président sea salt butter — with real sea salt kernels." So: This is not your common salted butter but butter with sea salt kernels. I see! And. of course, *real* sea salt kernels. Have you ever seen *unreal* sea salt kernels?

But it gets even better! On the back of the package it says: "Président sea salt butter is the high quality French butter for gourmets". I see! High-quality! French! And then for gourmets! Sounds good. Sound like a premium product. And gourmet? I certainly can identify with that.

Now to the small print: "It is produced in a small village in the middle of Normandy." Here I think immediately of Asterix and Obelix from the small Gallic village that does not want to surrender to the Roman Empire. Nice association. And I am also a bit of a rebel. Suits me.

"The use of real, hand-picked sea salt kernels…" Hand-picked? My head cinema develops pictures of children who have to sort salt kernels "… and the best cream gives this butter its smooth consistency…" Smooth consistency? When I take it out of the fridge, it is as solid as a rock! Nothing smooth here! "... and its extraordinary aroma." Man, it is salty. Just simply nice and salty.

"Its particular shape derives from the artisan traditions of French butter making." So... here I imagine more of an automatic assembly line production. How is that really going to make it to the supermarket refrigeration shelf in that quantity?

So much for the product. Another tip regarding the packaging: "Freshness cup for even more enjoyment." Hello? This is a plastic lid. Not more.

Conclusion: Perhaps I could now also excite you for this butter. But I am more concerned with the text and the associated effect. Apart from the excellent product, the copywriter deserves a medal. They created a premium product with their choice of words. They created many positive images and associations in my head. They were particularly clever in choosing the appropriate adjectives: "smooth, exceptional, special, craftmanship, etc."

Most salespeople underestimate the deliberate use of adjectives in communicating. The right wording is elementary.

TIP

"A good salesperson determines the pictures in the head of his customer" So: Make use of adjectives as magic words in selling. In a personal conversation as well as on the phone.

And: The butter costs more than two dollars at our supermarket and is the most expensive butter by far. This is what I call successful marketing.

Recently in California

There are lots of bars and restaurants in the road to the beach. But in front of one restaurant, there is a queue: Ten to twenty people are waiting to be seated at one of the sought-after tables. All other restaurants still have a lot of tables available. What is the difference?

It is a trattoria. Italian pasta dishes on the menu, a simple ambiance, and paper tablecloths dominate the picture. Like everywhere in the US, the waitrons are very friendly, pleasant and attentive. Portions are generous. And for just a little surcharge, one gets enormous portions. Who is supposed to eat all that? Well, no one wants to finish all of that but rather take the leftovers home. Doggy-Bag.

I do not have to mention that the food is delicious! I already assumed that with a queue like this. But apart from the portions and the taste, the guests can help themselves to wine. As often and as much as they want to. Afterward, the guests also state how much wine they consumed and what they want to pay for it. A deal based on trust.

Then the waitron hands out sheets of paper with an Italian song text. Shortly afterward, all the guests, together with the staff, sing the song at full volume. I have not experienced that yet either. A fantastic atmosphere.

Conclusion:

**Get your customers (or, in this case, your guests)
excited instead of only meeting their expectations!**

No matter what industry they belong to, every provider has to differentiate themselves from the competition positively. In my holiday example, quality and service were very good. This is similar to the competition. The special experience and the option concerning the product volume make the difference here.

What unexpected service do you offer to your customers? How do you differentiate yourself positively from the competition?

If you walk through life with your eyes open, you will always find a few good ideas, even in other industries, on how to stand out from your competitors.

System Catering and the Increased Flow of Saliva

At the restaurant: The waitress does not simply ask if anyone would like a dessert following the main course, but she comes to the table with a tray, puts it down, and presents a dozen sweet delights. At least three minutes pass while she is describing all the different desserts. Now, who is drooling after all? The post-sales rate is unbelievable! Until now, I only knew this from the HardRock Cafes: This franchise does system catering like for example McDonald's does. System catering means: Don't leave anything to chance!

What lesson can you learn from this for your sales?

Firstly: Don't just talk about what else the customer could buy in the context of cross-selling, but show it to him. You know already: A picture says more than a thousand words! Here are three examples from daily sales routines:

The sales representative that casually puts a small bottle of his chemical cleaner on the table during a customer visit. Quite visible, but he does not mention it specifically during the conversation. What happens? The customer gets curious and asks what it is. Usually only towards the end of the visit. Now the door to a conversation opens for the salesperson and the focus can be on the presentation. This is cross-selling in the truest sense of the word!

Or the bank consultant who puts a brochure on the table before a customer consultation. Right at the beginning of the meeting. Again, really casually. A flashy yellow post-it-sticker with the customer's name on it is visible on the brochure. Here, too, the customer will approach the object of curiosity on his own initiative.

I also remember my days as a trade representative: Often, I had promotional merchandise in my station wagon, and of course, I did not want to drive it around with me for days. I motivated myself and focused on the fact that the car had to be empty as fast as possible. So I just offered specifically these products. And when the customer would accompany me to the car at times, he would, of course, ask about the promotional merchandise.

Secondly: A system means to make "success independent of chance"!

Remember the example from Amazon.com: "Customers who bought this article also bought…" There are enough examples for industries that generate their main turnover from selective cross-selling.

Miracles in Sales: "I Will Tell You on the Evening before Your First Day at the Trade Show Whether Your Trade Show Will Be a Success!"

Miracles in Sales are very rare. But every now and then, they do happen…

During the previous week. An entrepreneur of a medium-sized company prepares for the next trade show. I am assisting him in it. Goal of the trade show: New customer acquisition. Architects and planners from the gardening and landscaping sector, as well as building material dealers have been identified as the target group.

"I will tell you on the evening before your first day at the trade show whether your trade show will be a success!"

The press often quotes my statement. In terms of context, it means that without fixed appointments with potential new customers at the trade show, you will only reach about 10% of the possible potential: namely, only the walk-in customers!

A study conducted by AUMA (Association of the German Trade Show Industry) years ago showed that 90% of a trade visitor's time at a trade show is already planned in advance with specific visits. So if you rely only on the visitor approach, you are usually doomed.

Back to the medium-sized company: The first step is a mailing. Three thousand two hundred trade show invitations to cold contacts. The usual response rate is below 1%. It can sometimes get up to 3% if it goes really (really!) well.

But in this case, a miracle happens.

A new advertising agency introduces itself and promises a response rate of more than 10%. Is that legitimate? My customer agrees that the advertiser guarantees him a response of at least 150 appointments. The advertiser agrees that if the response is less, he will pick up the phone and call the specific customers himself. Until 150 trade show appointments have been confirmed. I love such statements: A guarantee for new customers ;-)

An A3 letter without reinforcement, four-color printing, was sent out in an envelope with a large window on the back. The only thing really extraordinary: An individualized internet address to make contact.

The result: A week before the trade show, more than 800 customers had punched in the printed invitation link into their PCs. Of these, 330 made an appointment for the trade show electronically, including the time. At the same time, 280 indicated that they have a current pending project, for which the products of the company are interesting.

Wow!

I am impressed! So despite all the sensory overload, there are still real innovations in acquisition. Compliments!

"You Should Not Run after Every Ball. You Have to Anticipate Where the Ball Is Going and Then Be There Already." (Franz Beckenbauer)

There was another one of my son's soccer games on the weekend. Once again, it soon became apparent what the coach's biggest challenge with the six to seven-year-old players was: The positional play. I got the impression that there is a genetic code in the boys' heads that says: Ball = go and kick! On the field, this meant that packs were permanently formed. Wherever the ball was, all (!) the field players were, too. The main task of the coaches of both teams was to direct the players back to the right position.

There is also positional play in sales.

Only... how should a salesperson anticipate where the ball is going? The approach: A suitable and well-maintained CRM program with data the salesperson interprets correctly.

The right moment means: Having a suitable follow-up and getting to the customer at the right moment. For example, the customer said in the past that he has entered into supplier contracts for 2013. When asked when he would start planning for 2014, he confirmed the month of September. So: Follow-up on 1 September 2013.

Or you consider the industry standard for follow-up dates: The beginning or the end of the season, leading trade shows, financial years, legislation amendments, quality and delivery problems of the competition, changes of employees in key positions, etc.

In my sector of sales training, large enterprises start planning from September for the next year. If we only phone in November, we will be put off to the next year. You can only blame yourself then.

With the right customer means: Prioritize: A, B, C customers Define the relevant criteria which make up these customer categories. This is very (!) individual. It may be that you take into account sales, contribution margin, potential, creditworthiness, support effort, etc. Like I said: it is very individual! The next step would be to find out specific data of the customers according to your criteria. Now you have the sequence in which to proceed.

To be well-prepared means: "I was just in the area" or "I haven't seen him in a while" are no valid reasons to contact a customer. Do your homework!

1. Retrospective: What have you achieved with this specific customer in the past?

2. Present situation: What is the customer or his industry concerned about?

3. In future: Where do you want to go with your customer?

4. Keyword goals: Set a google alert in the news function for your customer and his industry to be informed in time.

With the right offer means: You should have already prepared your quotation. Ideally, with some alternatives, depending on the situation. Start with new ideas and products for your existing customer base before asking them for their regular requirements.

Please remember: Grass does not grow faster just because you pull it. That means sales does not only mean diligence but also a certain acquisition and sales intelligence.

What Athletes Know and Salespeople Would Like To Know!

After a talk, one of the participants comes to me and gives me an autograph card instead of a business card. An autograph card? The man's name is Pasquale Passarelli. He won a gold medal at the 1984 Olympics. Fine, but today he looks very different from the man in the picture. His physical condition is also significantly worse. But he is a very successful salesperson today. We talk about his sporting success and about the fact that former athletes are often better salespeople.

> ## TIP
>
> **Those who have learned early on in sports to organize themselves, motivate themselves, and deal with victories and defeats, will have a much easier time as salespeople since many aspects of everyday sports life are also reflected in everyday sales life.**

There are also some colleagues in the trainer and speaker community who were very successful as competitive athletes at a young age. Motivational and personality trainer Jörg Löhr was a multiple national handball player, sales trainer Karsten Brocke was a German champion in motocross, and motivational trainer Christian Bischoff was a professional basketball player.

Contacts Only Hurt Those Who Don't Have Any!

A favorite question of journalists is: What has changed in sales lately? And yes, there are always a few little things that change. Although these are usually not fundamentally new communication channels. No, it is rather the fine-tuning.

A few years ago, Joachim Rumohr, the number 1 XING expert, and I published an audiobook about the acquisition of new customers via XING. Acquisition engine XING.

At that time. I had recommended a phrase for the direct approach: "Contacts only hurt those who don't have any!" If you are active with this phrase today, you will immediately be identified as a so-called contact collector by your counterparts. This phrase is being used too much, too often these days. Please delete!!!

In addition, event invitations were still an acquisition engine for webinars and seminars in 2009. Response rates were often in the double-digit percentage range. Today, it is a one-way street: I do not even delete all the invitations anymore because it is too tedious. Forget about this communication channel!

These are only two examples of changes in the way we use XING. It is also good to know that the XING AG has carried out technical changes.

For this reason, Joachim Rumohr and I have perfected the audiobook and the multimedia DVD. The user of the audio book *Acquisition Engine XING* as well as those who would like to get more in-depth knowledge on the subject, can work specifically with the new version 2.0.

My latest conclusion about *Acquisition Engine XING*: It is a tool that is of great use in many areas of new customer acquisition and professional sales. A hammer is also a tool. It is obvious that the hammer is most suitable for driving in nails. For screws, there are better tools. The same applies to XING. There are certain areas in sales in which XING is indispensable in my everyday life. These are, e.g., the preparation of the first customer contact or as a source of information for referrals. But: There are areas in which other tools are a lot better suited.

A skilled craftsman always has several options to optimally use his tools.

With this in mind, I wish you a really good command of your sales tools to leverage your maximum potential.

Value and Price

Why are wind turbines from Enercon up to 20% more expensive than those of the competition? And how is it possible under the circumstances that Enercon holds a market share of 60% in Germany?

How can Miele be so successful in selling washing machines if they are about 20% above the prices of the other suppliers?

Why was Gillette in a position to ask for 50% more on introducing its triple razor blade at the time?

In advance: The answer to these three questions is always the same! Independent of the fact whether it is end costumer or business customers sales. And these products are really not sexy. They are also not status symbols or products that follow a fashion trend.

I was able to make an interesting observation at Professor Hermann Simon, Head of the management consultancy Simon-

Kucher & Partners: He studied the Latin word *pretium*. The word means "price": In other words, the sum of money that the ancient Romans already wanted for a service or goods. So far, so good. But *pretium* also means *value*. This is exciting: Even the ancient Romans knew that a certain price also meant a certain value.

Pretium = Price = Value

The price is usually set by the provider. Okay. The value is then in turn set by the customer. The individual benefit for the customer. And that brings us to marketing and sales. The main task of these two areas is to communicate the service, the value for the customer. Because only the communicated performance, the conveyed value for the customer, counts. You can offer the best product. But if you are not able to communicate the (added) value to your customer, you will never achieve high prices.

Enercon, for example, offers economic benefits to customers for its wind turbines by offering more contracts at a much higher availability. And Miele washing machines simply last much longer than any other supplier's models.

This teaches us that we always have to look at the value of our offer first before we go into pricing.

We create value through innovation, quality, economy, design, service, and system integration. We communicate value through appropriate positioning, brand policy, packaging, presentation, brand environment, advertising, argumentation. But above all, through salespeople who stand behind their offer, are enthusiastic about it and have learned to communicate the performance.

TIP

There are no prices that are too high, only offers with too little performance. Or salespeople who are unable to communicate this performance to their customers properly.

With this in mind: Price = communicated value.

Is Cold Calling Still in Fashion? Or: Why My Aunt Should Have Called Beforehand.

On Monday morning, four applicants who had applied for the position of sales trainer, came to our offices. Everyone was to present themselves and a sales subject in form of a talk. Trainer casting by the hour. After the second presentation, my assistant told me that my aunt had just been here. She would return at 01:00 p.m.

My aunt is a pensioner and lives in Cologne. Unannounced! And now, she was kept waiting for three hours. Or rather: Shopping in the city of Bochum. I did not know why she came to see me. Did she just want to say "hello"? Now I felt bad for keeping her waiting.

She just wanted to visit me in the office. She was lucky, taking into account how seldom I am actually in the office.

Exciting, because she had never done this before. I wanted to be polite and invited her for lunch. A nice meeting, but not really that relaxed. I had an extremely busy schedule on that day, filled with appointments and tasks. I was not really here nor there. An hour later, it was back to the daily business for me. This hour was now missing in my day.

If she had only said something beforehand, I could have planned my day around it. And everything would have been fine.

I would guess the information so far is not that exciting for you. But what if you translate this topic into "cold calling for new customer acquisition or at existing customers." Is this approach still in fashion?

Why do salespeople still make cold calls?

1. Because the boss has set call targets. Every day a certain number of calls have to be done. Success on the basis of: "Much helps much." What is the result? Customers are being visited without an appointment just to fulfill the target. It does not get any results but soothes the conscience, the boss and the statistic. And here the question arises: What are you being paid for? For visits or for orders? For the intention or the effect?

2. Because the salesperson can use the day more flexibly. They can decide on what to do and who to visit on the spur of the moment. And that way, they do not have to prepare diligently for the visit either.

3. Because the sales representative simply is not good at telephone acquisition. The principle applies: If you are a strong salesperson in a face-to-face conversation, i.e., during a visit, you are far from being strong on the phone. But if you are strong on the phone, you will, in most cases, also be strong in a face-to-face conversation. And it is precisely for this reason

because many salespeople are afraid of simply being rejected on the phone, that no appointments are made in advance by telephone.

What speaks in favor of customer visits with prior telephone appointments?

From the point of view of the salesperson:

1. The success rate is drastically higher because the customer is there at the agreed time and takes time for the conversation.

2. Waiting times at the customer's are significantly reduced. You gain time.

3. The salesperson is valued significantly higher. You are being expected!

4. The order rate is much higher because the customer is prepared and can make decisions at shorter notice: Visit by Appointment = Order!

5. The average order value is significantly higher because you can better assess the customer's needs and situation in advance via the internet and CRM. Upselling and cross-selling are now much more successful.

From the point of view of the customer (or from my point of view when my aunt came to visit me):

1. The customer can also plan his time.

2. The customer can anticipate and prepare for the visit. This significantly improves the conversation quality, and decisions about projects and orders can be made quicker.

3. The value placed on the customer is higher. With phrases like "I was just in the neighbourhood, so I thought I'd stop by…" you are indirectly telling the customer that you are not going out of your way for them.

TIP

Conclusion: Less but in better quality is more here. More value. And this is the difference between a pro and an amateur!

If you want to significantly increase your success rate once again, then also use these two tried-and-tested strategy tips:

1. Not only make the appointment by phone, but also arrange the time necessary: "In order for you to get a first concrete overview, we will only need 45 minutes. Would that suit you, Mr./Ms. Customer?" Also verify the time budget at the beginning of the visit. "Mr./Ms. Customer, we had arranged on the phone that we would be finished by 04:00 p.m. Is that still okay for you?" Now you increase your chances of success even more significantly, when you mention the three most important subjects of the meeting while arranging the

appointment. The customer knows now what to expect and can prepare accordingly.

2. Confirm the appointment after the phone call in writing: Depending on your target group, via letter (end customer/private customer), email (technology-oriented business customers) or fax (has the highest effect on the attention of customers who still receive it as a paper fax). You confirm in it the time, duration, participants and the three main subjects of the meeting. Alternatively, you can ask your customer to bring certain information to the meeting (e.g., inventory, requirements) in order to be able to decide quicker. It has also proven effective with new customer visits to send links about your company, who you are and what you have to offer. Most customers would like to know in advance who is coming to visit them. Especially by confirming your appointment in writing, you clearly stand out from your competition and give your customer the feeling that you are a professional.

If you work in sales, you do not live from customer visits, but from sales.

And I can really look forward to my aunt's next visit... and be prepared ;-)

Acquisition Appointment Arranged: And Now What?

Congratulations! You have arranged for a first visit with a potential customer. With that, you have already passed the first obstacle (I know this is being subjective. But most salespeople find the biggest challenge in arranging an appointment with a target customer in the first place!). And now what?

1. Of course you confirm the appointment via e-mail (without an Outlook appointment!), via fax or for via letter (without enclosures) for end customer business: Thank you, day, time, subjects, estimated duration, a website for information, participants, necessary documents…

2. Find the contact person via XING or, for international business, via LinkedIn. Send an individual, nice contact request to link up: 1. Value: Your contact person sees that you are interested in them and that you prepare well. 2. When they confirm, you receive further information via their profiles. The most important in my opinion is: Their contacts! I can see who they know and whom of these people I know (similarities attract). In addition, I can see who else I would like to get to know (referral marketing). Often, I then also see who the competitors are and can prepare myself even better.

3. You find this too offensive? You would only send a contact request after the personal meeting? Well, your contact can confirm your request later or even decline it.

4. What are the interests of your target customer? This you can also find in their profiles on XING and LinkedIn. The groups they belong to in both networks also give background and information about their interests. A nice side effect is that

you can often find more interesting new customer contacts ("People always move in the same circles").

5. "Business is about people." Therefore, also use the "soft facts" for interesting small talk while getting to know each other.

6. It goes without saying that all information is to be stored in the CRM program.

7. If there are several weeks between making the appointment and the actual meeting, you should find a reason to contact the person shortly before the meeting to confirm the appointment.

For the brave ones among you: An American colleague adds the contact directly into his newsletter distribution list, sends them his latest e-book and then a short mobile phone video, in which

he expresses his enthusiasm for the meeting.

The largest team I ever managed consisted of 14 employees in my own team. But I was able to observe in numerous projects, how salespeople were managed extremely well or extremely badly and what influence good leadership has on people, customers and turnover. I wish you lots of fun with the following examples around the subject of leadership in sales.

Sometimes We Pitch. And You?

"Dad, what is experience?"

"... that is when ..."

Motocross. Sunday morning. As usual, I want to be amongst the first to be on the track. There is more room at that time and the surface is still fresh.

10:00 a.m. Let's go.

Due to permanent rainfall over the last few days, the course is slippery. Not one second of decent driving. I am getting cramps in my forearms. At least there is a lot of room on the track.

After three rounds: Pitstop. The paddock is crowded. But hardly anyone leaves to go on the track. Hmm ...!?

After an hour, the track has been run dry. Now it is more fun again.

And again, I have learned something: The early bird ... uuhhmm ... the early driver — drives in the mud!

"... this is what is called experience!"

And what can you take home from this for your sales? Experience!

So: Sometimes, we pitch. And you?

During a pitch, the customer has several salespeople competing with each other. The salespeople present their individual solutions for the same task. The customer can then perfectly compare the offers. This type of contest is particularly liked by architects and advertising agencies and has almost become an industry-standard.

How can you optimize your opportunities to win orders in this particular sales situation?

We always want to be the last to present. We do everything to be the last of all salespeople in the pitch. Sometimes, we don't even go if we are not the last ones. Why? The customer learns with every presentation. They can be more critical and ask more questions each time. When it is our turn then, they know exactly what to look out for.

TIP

Now we can answer all their questions and, at the same time, place new ideas, arguments and questions ("Geistige Brandstiftung®") with the customer and thus distinguish ourselves. Moreover, the last one remains most strongly in the memory.
Being present in the customer's mind!

Even more important to me is a commitment from the customer after our presentation. With the last one, the customer has little chance of the excuse: "We can't decide yet. We have to see everyone first." The last one can usually go much stronger into the commitment: Often, we know where we stand at the end.

So: The early bird … uuhhmm … the first salesperson will have difficulty in getting the order through a pitch!

Bad Losers

"I have decided to never give up", says Alex Ferguson, a legend among soccer coaches.

Of course, he wanted to see this inner attitude from his players as well. Therefore, he recruited players for his team who were seen as *bad losers* and asked them to work extremely hard. Over the years, this attitude became infectious: The pros themselves did not take well to co-players who did not give everything. This also applied to the biggest stars in the team.

Five remarks on this:

1. In the January 2014 issue of *Harvard Business Manager*, you will find an exciting report on the "Ferguson formula": Eight lessons that can be applied to management. A must-read for managers and soccer enthusiasts alike.

"The limits of the athlete are the limits in the mind of the coach."

2. This statement comes from Austrian sports psychologist Markus Schnitzler. It is a good match for the scene described above. Ferguson transfers his inner attitude to his players. The coach and his attitude are often the limiting factor. The same applies to sales management!

3. Find salespeople who are bad losers! Selling can be trained. Changing one's own attitude is significantly more difficult. If you have a "farmer" sales force focusing on repeat customers, this is important. If you have a "hunter" sales force focusing on new business, then this is the basic requirement for above-average sales success.

4. Prof. Dr. Jörg Knoblauch says that A employees want an A environment; C employees want a C environment. An A-employee in a C-environment will leave soon again and vice versa. I say the same goes for hunters and farmers: A hunter wants a hunter-friendly environment. He will never be happy in a farmer's organization. Again, you can find the parallel to the Ferguson formula.

5. As a sales manager, you will be responsible for selecting/recruiting the right players/salespeople and creating the right environment to enable the greatest success. YOU ARE RESPONSIBLE! NO ONE ELSE!

Oh yes. Another two athletes who could not lose:

Boris Becker was promoted because he caught the scout's eye during a youth screening. Not because he was stronger or better, but because of his attitude!

Oliver Kahn. Okay, I don't have to explain here what I am getting at. Anyone who has ever seen him as a goalkeeper in a game where his team was behind knows what I am getting at. Must-read: *Ich. Erfolg kommt von innen.* [Me. Success comes from within.]

"I Am Not Looking for New Salespeople!" … and the Earth Is flat!

"You do not only get paid for what you do, but also for what you don't do!" … and this particularly applies to managers in sales!

You are not looking for new salespeople? Your team is complete? Are you sure?

Two thoughts on this:

Thought number 1: You always have a basic fluctuation in a sales team: Pregnancy, parental leave, sickness, burnout, dismissals, retirement.

As manager it is your task therefore to constantly make sure that you have replacements. You know the turmoil in the market when you don't have an area covered! And this is exactly what your competition is waiting for!

A few basic principles from the soccer clubs of the major leagues can be learnt: A team here also does not arrive with exactly 11 players. There are always a few substitutes. And the squad of a team usually consists of more than double the number of eleven players!

How many "substitute players" do you have for your sales team?

Or do you think that the gap left by a missing player is easy to fill? How long does your hiring and onboarding process take?

1. Drawing up a list of requirements

2. Composing advertisement and posting online

3. Collecting and compiling applications (four weeks? eight weeks?)

4. Job interviews, tests, trial work (four or eight weeks?)

5. Employment contract

6. Taking into consideration notice period of the applicant (four weeks or three months to the end of a quarter?)

7. Induction (How systematic is this process in your company? Six months or even a year before the salesperson reaches "cruising speed"?)

… and what happens if the candidate leaves again? Or when you have made the wrong choice and now have to find a new candidate?

But let us assume that these points are not relevant for YOU.

Then we are still left with the second thought: In a team of ten salespeople, you will always have two or three who do not perform according to your expectations. If the issue here is not *cannot* but *don't want to,* you should replace them! If you do not have replacement staff however, you will not exchange them. You will wait it out. You hope that the salesperson will still have some inspiration and improve his/her performance. Well, hope floats…

"You do not only get paid for what you do, but also for what you don't do!"

My tip: It is better to act than to react! Build up a team of substitutes for the long term! Always have a few substitutes waiting on the bench! Always have an alternative course of action at hand! Never become dependent! Never give the competition a gap! Recognize recruiting as one of your core tasks and make it one of your core competencies!

Not Good in a Team? Do Loners Make Better Salespeople?

"I was always amazed at how other salespeople in the car dealership where I worked would stand around in small groups every morning and chat. For obvious reasons, I want to call this an "info circle". I was a loner and kept to myself.

When I showed up for work, I thought it was pointless wasting my time by joining their chats. After all, they did not want to buy a car from me! And apart from that, I did not get up in the morning to gossip. I did not have the time to listen to any of their jokes and I did not spend my lunch break with the other colleagues.

It was my job to sell cars and I did not feel like listening all day to the other salespeople griping.'

These are the words of the best car salesperson on the planet: Joe Girard. For 15 consecutive years he was listed as the best salesperson in the Guinness Book of Records. During this time he sold 13,000 cars — an average of six cars per day. Every day!

In a review by Amazon I read that one cannot learn anything from him, because after all, as a salesperson he was a loner. Uh-huh.

Is that really so? Do salespeople work more successfully in a team? It depends on the task. A key account manager who has to come up with complex solutions can only be successful in a team. Correct: A team is needed on the sales side: the longer the sales cycle is, the more complex the solution, the more extensive the aftersales service, the higher the consultancy effort and the more extensive the buying center on the customer side is. But this is only the case in B2B (business to business) business and is not all that common. Most sales agreements have a much simpler structure. Especially in the retail/consumer business.

It follows thus: Apart from the abovementioned exceptions, the subject of top salespeople's ability to work in a team is highly overrated then!

Just because teamwork is currently in vogue does not mean that it needs to be listed as a requirement in every job advertisement for salespeople!

Conclusion:

1. As a manager you should also look for the loner, depending on the task at hand.

2. As salesperson you should focus on what you are being paid to do: Concluding sales, turnover, success. Optimize your active selling time. Concentrate on your income generating time. Social wellness is important, but only to a limited extent. Your clients and your commission pay your salary, not your co-workers. Don't let negative office gossip demotivate you. Follow your goals!

We Wanted Our Salespeople to Be Young, Naïve, Hungry and Stupid.

It is salespeople who keep the wheels of the economy turning worldwide. Nothing happens on this planet without somebody selling something to somebody. And yet the job of a salesperson does not have a good image in our culture.

So when a courageous man in Hollywood is prepared to make a film about salespeople and show this in cinemas, it must be something special!

Personally I enjoy films such as *Boiler Room, Wall Street* or *The Wolf of Wall Street.* How about you?

If you are like me you will like this quote from Jordan Belfort, the protagonist from *The Wolf of Wall Street.* Have fun with these…

Belfort about the subject of recruiting … "To find the best salespeople":

"At Stratton we do the mirror test with our applicants — that means, we tie a mirror under the nose of the applicant and wait until it mists up. When the mirror misted up, we employed the applicant, when the mirror did not mist up it meant the applicant was dead, and that was the only reason for us not hiring this person …"

Belfort about the topic of applicant qualifications:

"We wanted our salespeople to be young, naïve, hungry and stupid. [...] Give me someone like that and I will make them rich without any problems. But if you give me somebody with intelligence and an imagination — well, that will be a bit more difficult."

Belfort about the topic of "viewpoint — inner attitude":

"There were no sales areas, no advertising brochures, no existing customers, no salary; it was all purely on commission. "We are cold calling machines", he whistled, [...]. "That is why we make so much money."

"There is something I can definitely tell you about the penguin: he is a stubborn idiot. He would waddle from door to door, knock and knock until his knuckles bled, while fighting to hold back his tears. But he made an average commission of 300 dollars per day, that was worth a few tears."

Belfort about the subject of the target group:

"[...], as everyone was only looking at the price, I thought: Why don't we try and sell to rich people?"

Belfort to "What is selling":

"I had managed to flog off an ice cream on the beach before, but that was not real selling; it was more about working hard and having success."

How important is motivation?

"You know what, motivation is really important. Without it, your sales staff withers away and reaches its breaking point faster than you think."

Does one get born to be a salesperson?

"[...] So I started training the salespeople and I realized that I had a knack for it. To be exact, I did it so well that I could have taken any guy from the street and turned him into a meat salesman."

Cold calling...

"It was my job to establish customer contacts, and that is the worst job on Wall Street. I would dial phone numbers all day long trying to get past the secretaries of wealthy businesspeople. I was thoroughly tested and had to swallow my pride — but in the end I could do nothing else but make the best of it. The only thing that kept me going was the hope for a better future."

Belfort on the subject of "preparation" and "call script":

"The most important thing when selling is that you learn to read from the script making it sound as if you are not reading from a script. [...] Just pretend you are an actor on a stage: Pitch your voice high and then bring it down again; speak fast and then slower again. This way you keep your customers interested and ensure that they listen to you attentively. And don't even think about picking up the phone until you have answers to all conceivable objections."

Do resubmissions and follow-up calls make sense?

"You work with logic and reason and massive pressure. [...] We - do - not - work - with follow-up - calls! This means you only have one chance with these people. So stick exactly to the script."

Lone fighter or team?

"The first thing Pizarro did when he reached the New World, was to burn all his stupid ships so that his team had no other choice but to create an existence in the New World. And I want you to do exactly the same. I want you to cut off all your escape routes! [...] That is where our strength comes from: It is based on community, on a common effort, on the united energy in this room, the most motivated people Wall Street has ever seen. This is a room of winners".

Now... What do you think... Do you agree that there is a mind-set and principles which made salespeople successful 20 years ago which are still valid today? I think so.

9/11, the First Day at a school, the First Day at Work

Do you still remember where you were on 11 September 2001? Do you still remember your first day at school?... and how was your first day at work with your current employer?

Some days are literally burnt into your memory forever! Regardless whether they are positive or negative.

I will never forget my first week in the field. August 1990. For one day I was allowed to accompany an experienced colleague on a customer visit. Then the Opel Kadett station wagon stood in front of the door, I was given a list of customers and turnover, a sample collection and a motivating "Wishing you success". My travel area covered the postal codes 1 and 2: Berlin and Northern Germany. In my structured manner I chose the area furthest to the west in my region: One week Oldenburg, Wilhelmshaven, Aurich, Emden, Leer… conscientiously I visited (visited!!!) EVERY client on my list. The result: by Friday night I had not written up a single order. Self-doubt! Frustration!

It is not only that day which has burnt itself into my memory, but actually the whole week! What would I have given to have the knowledge and ability that I have now for that task!

Many salespeople in the field share this experience with me. In small and medium-sized enterprises this is the norm rather than the exception! Did you know that 80% of those who give notice during their probation period have made that decision already on their first day? Or that 39% already leave the company again in the first 90 days (study of Harvey Nash)?

Well… for my it was my great love. For nine years. But it was not "love at first sight". The start could really have been easier.

If you are a manager in sales, it is worth thinking about this: How much money, time and frustration could you save with an optimal induction process, in current terminology: "onboarding"! For all affected parties: employers, employees, customers and colleagues!

TIP

Sales onboarding comprises the time period from signing the employment contract to the end of the probation period. The most sensitive period of collaboration between the manager and the salesperson.

It is just not enough to greet the new employee on their first day with words like these: "Oh! You're the new one? Is it the first of the month already? Oh well, let's see what we can do with you." ... even if this is rather the norm than the exception in small and medium-sized enterprises.

I Made a Mistake!

One of the less pleasant moments in the life of a manager is to give notice to an employee. To congratulate an applicant to a new job is a wonderful moment for both parties. But to give notice to somebody is exactly the opposite!

On Monday I had to give notice to a new employee after only 17 days. Why? It wasn't going to work. And I did not see this beforehand. I made a mistake. A mistake during the selection process.

How was this possible? After all, my selection process is extremely diligent: A very detailed requirements profile which makes most interested persons see that they are not suitable for the job. Then the shortlisting of applicants involving an extremely high degree of rejections. After this, telephonic interviews with candidates lasting as long as 30 minutes, where I ask pointed questions and listen very attentively. After this, candidates that seem suitable are invited to a well-designed trial session with my team and myself.

During the last year we had 16 candidates in the trial session. Divided over three dates. Three times the daily business had to come to a standstill for a few hours. Not to think of the costs for the process. And especially not of the costs for all the job advertisements!

This whole effort resulted in having two candidates sign an employment contract. That is the pleasant moment for both sides as described above.

But unfortunately, it then becomes apparent that the required willingness to perform is not present and that the desired ability to learn which would ensure having a successful future in my team is just not there. Too bad. My mistake!

I console myself with the statement from Jack Welch, the most successful manager of the last decade and ex-GE-boss, that even managers with decades-long experience have a success rate of three out of four *(WirtschaftsWoche 5/2007)*.

Should I have given the employee more time after two frank performance reviews and providing clear guidelines? Are 17 days enough to make the correct decision? Clearly some skills improve with time. But the main reason has nothing to do with ability, in other words the "can", but with the willingness, in other words, "wanting to". And as employer, I do not have much influence on the willingness of a candidate.

The Americans accuse us Germans of being "too fast to hire" and "too slow to fire". This is food for thought.

Rather make a cut now, then having to have *that* talk with a disappointed seminar participants. True to the motto: What will it cost me if I do not do it?

Yes, they do exist: The trainers in my team who have successfully passed the requirements process and who have surpassed my expectations and those of the customers for years! The second new recruit also moves into that direction.

So: Proceed with posing maximum quality requirements for candidates while at the same time optimizing the process. Once again, I have learnt something.

12:1 — Or How to Demotivate a Salesperson

Have you heard about the 12:1 idea from Switzerland? "The highest wage paid by a business may not exceed 12 times the lowest wage paid by the same undertaking…"

What do you think would happen if you applied this rule for sales? Maybe not much would happen to "farmers' who concentrate more on taking care of customers and mostly have a very small variable in their income. But what would happen to the "hunters", who concentrate more on bringing in new business and who generally have a component in their remuneration which largely depends on their success?

A wise saying of managers is this: As a manager you cannot motivate a salesperson. You can only ensure that they do not get demotivated.

"Hunters" with above average performance would only be demotivated with capping of income and they would immediately look for a new field of activity in their profession. These type of salespeople want to determine their income, want to be judged by their own performance and do not want to be hindered by regulations stemming from envy.

This makes me think of an interesting situation from the past: Before a sales training session, the manager gives me a brief about the group: "Mr. Kreuter, in this group there are three participants who as sales representative clearly earn more in the field than I earn as managing director. And that is fine with me."

My perception about this business: A hunter style sales business, very successful, with a manager who knows how sales work.

Conclusion:

1. Good that the Swiss have rejected the 12:1 idea (by the way, the opposing side has worked strongly with "spiritual arson").

2. As manager in sales you can achieve much with targets and money... Both with regard to success as well as failure.

Is That Really What You Want? Are You Sure?

"The prospect of leadership positions" is one of the two most important performance incentives for sales employees. That was the finding of the current study *DVS-Vertriebsmonitor*

2013/2014 [DVS Sales Monitor 2013/14]. I wonder whether the interviewed salespeople really knew what they wanted there?

Do you know what a player coach is?

> "A player coach is a person who trains a sports team, but at the same time has the right to join the team as a player…
>
> Player coaches are mostly older, more experienced players, who at the end of their career exchange their active career as soccer players with that of a coach, but also still play for a while…
>
> In the German major league, you cannot be a player coach anymore."
>
> *Source: Wikipedia*

Most salespeople in small and medium-sized enterprises are active as "player coaches". They spend an unbelievable amount of time with the customer and enjoy shooting goals all the time instead of concentrating on the leadership or trainer role. This behavior is justified with the alibi of "being close to the customer". Nonsense!

In a study prof. Karl Pinczolits from the University of Applied Sciences Wiener Neustadt describes why there are so many player coaches in sales (which, by the way, are not found in other management areas): Managers do not get any recognition!

Yes, you read that right:

Conclusion:

1. There are no player coaches in the major league! Player
   coaches are found in the district league! Where does your
   business play regarding sales.

2. I have met some sales executives who would much rather be
   on the road again as salespeople: Recognition and working
   independently is what they miss the most! They would much
   rather be on the road working operationally again with their
   customers than sitting in the office with admin issues or sit
   in meetings or get aggravated as go-between between management and the sales team.

3. Making the best salesperson the sales manager? In many
   cases this means that the business now loses the best source
   of revenue and gains a mediocre manager. Why? Because
   managing sales employees is something completely different from motivating customers to make a decision to pur-

chase! Managing is a job in itself and has to be learnt, to say it in the words of Prof. Fedmund Malik.

So: Is that really what you want? Are you sure?

Finding Instead of Searching: Salesperson Recruiting With a T-Shirt and the Alternative

In a recent study, the recruitment agency Manpower has come up with some interesting figures:

TIP

**52% of those surveyed are satisfied with their job.
30% would recommend their job to a friend.
43% would like to change their job immediately
or within the next year.**

These findings immediately make me think of the subject of recruiting in sales. Because … if you apply these figures to a sales team, then you as a manager have a real problem. When so many employees are thinking of "jumping ship", it means that they are already not performing at 100% capacity. At the same time, it is becoming increasingly difficult to find good salespeople. It also does not make a difference whether an employee works in the field or in-house. Good salespeople don't just grow on trees!

What this could lead to: A few days ago, a participant displayed his current need for employees in sales at an event for salespeople with a T-shirt especially printed for this purpose.

Yes — I also asked myself whether this could work? I did not have the chance to speak to him, but various people told me of situations where participants passed their business cards to the gentleman. Openly or secretly. So there they are: the 43% from the survey.

Conclusion: It is becoming more and more difficult to find TOP salespeople!

A better way: If you think that the option with the T-shirt does not suit you and your business, there are of course a dozen better ways for you!

And… yes! Yes, they do exist: the TOP salespeople! You just have to know how and where to find them!

A Trained Donkey Is Not a Racehorse!

My two trainers and I turn consultants into salespeople. We turn salespeople into TOP salespeople! But if you send us a donkey, we will return a trained donkey to you, even if you expect getting back a racehorse!

With this I want to say: If a manager has made a mistake with staff recruitment, it is difficult to fix this mistake by taking measures for further training.

A few days ago, in a workshop for sales managers, we were given the following task: How can we bring our salesperson to perform even better?

It became apparent that the list of requirements for new applicants was designed by the human resources department some time ago. They were actually looking for professional consultants for the retail sector. Farmers. Relationship managers.

But in the workshop, it became more and more obvious: The company needs hunters. Salespeople in the retail sector, who can sell at high prices. Mostly once-off sales. With a short sales cycle. Excellent in concluding a deal. And should it happen that at some stage there is no customer in the shop, potential clients must be rung up. So — also good with tele sales.

The list of requirements and the real needs were exactly the opposite of each other!

To close this gap with training now takes enormous effort or is nearly impossible — even if we earn our money with this!

Conclusion of the workshop:
The correct employees
(hunters — a short sales cycle)
+ hit rate
(customer appointments in the shop and telephone calls)
+ hit impact
(proven strength in closing deals)
= maximum sales success!

An insight for you from this: First define what type of salesperson you really need! Find the right employee! Only then does training make sense!

This Is Not a Wailing Wall! Everyone Needs to Feel Better Afterwards than Before!

Did you know that most visitors on online job markets are active on Mondays at around 11:00 a.m.? You come back from a lovely weekend and realize: this does not make me happy!

With salespeople it is often at a different time: shortly after a sales meeting! That is when many salespeople know: this does not make me happy!

Why? Because many sales meetings are used as a wailing wall where everyone has something to complain about and some individual fates are discussed into the finest detail which actually does not interest the majority at all. And often also because the numbers do not add up and the manager uses the occasion to really dish it out.

And who is responsible for this? The manager I think!

Dear managers in sales,
You cannot motivate your employees. They were already highly motivated when they signed the contract. You can only ensure that they do not get demotivated! And that is exactly why the sales meeting is such an important management tool in sales: Here you can strongly influence the mood of your salespeople!

Ensure that every salesperson feels better after the meeting than before the meeting! This is your job!

A few thoughts on this:

- Is Friday afternoon really the best time for a sales meeting? If the meeting results in frustration, the employees take this with them into the weekend! If the result is wanting to gain new customers, they must wait two days before they can start.

- Is your own board room always the best venue? Get out of the daily business environment! Concentration! There are different, more pleasant places, where the participants do not still have to sort out upcoming issues during breaks.

- Start each meeting with positive subject matter. Participants can, for example, share one to three successful experiences. Experiences that make them proud: New customers acquired, gaining back old customers, actions, turnover… successes! Always start like this and turn this into a ritual!

- Let individual employees show how certain successes were achieved with specific products or with special customers. Best practice! Learning with each other, from each other.

- Practice arguments, preparing or dealing with objections or sales techniques. Those who do not want to improve, are not really good!

- Deal with successful businesses or personalities. What can your team learn from the examples? What are they doing better? Where are they better?

- Don't go through the numbers as a collective. Every employee can do this on their own when you send them the figures. Don't discuss individual cases. Figures are discussed in one-on-one meetings. And by the way, that also applies to criticism!

- Delete the item "General" from your agenda! Items that are not on the agenda, should not be discussed! If salespeople want to get clarity on an issue, they can ask to have this included on the agenda a few days before the meeting. But it is your decision what is included on the agenda. Inform your employees about the topics of the meeting by sending out the agenda in advance and tell them what individual preparation you expect from each participant. Then there will be no unplanned surprises on both sides!

- Close off punctually! 06:00 p.m. on the agenda means the meeting closes at 06:00 p.m.!

A sales meeting is an energy refueling station for everybody in the team. Everyone has to feel better afterwards than before the meeting!

Salespeople get the confirmation that they are with the right company and the right manager; managers get the confirmation that they have the right employees in the team.

The sport psychologist Markus Schnitzler says: "I know whether a team is a winning team or a losing team. This has to do with the topic of conversation is in the change room: is it about success or about what doesn't work?" What does your team talk about?

Note: Yes, I know, the subject is more complex than this! But these are acquisition stimuli and not a manual! And yes, it works! I know sales managers who inspire their team time and again with this management tool and thereby achieve "extreme turnover"! And yes, managing can also be learnt!

Make or Buy? — Young Talent in Sales

During an award ceremony Dietrich Mateschitz, the founder and principal of Red Bull, was asked whether he works with consultants. He confirmed that he indeed uses personnel consultants extensively. Why? Because his market is growing so quickly, that he has not got enough time to train his skilled workers himself. He wants employees that are already "fit", even if it costs him more.

Dietrich Mateschitz has no choice. But most businesses do …

For many years we have been offering a seminar together with an industry association, which my trainer Denise Spekowius conducts with great success: "Selling for apprentices — sales knowledge that starts where the vocational school ends — awaken the sales talent of your apprentices". This association has recognized that professional knowledge alone is not enough for up-and-coming salespeople. That is why the seminar is fully booked every year.

As the manager, which alternatives have I really got? It therefore makes sense to inspire young talent early on for sales. Or to check whether sales is actually something that the candidates can see themselves in for the long term. Most candidates have a false idea or no idea of sales! That needs to be corrected early on.

And now an interesting anecdote: The head of a development program for managers from an international company tells me that he hands out a certificate from a renowned university to his employees at the end of the training program. He thereby wants to capture their further training "in black and white"... so that the participants have something in their hands.

I strongly advised him not to do this: These certificates only encourage employees to switch their workplace! Training is good and important! But the certificate is counterproductive for the company!

And this is when he remembered: He himself changed jobs many years ago from the company who had enabled him to get his MBA certificate only a few months after he passed the examination. These days there are no more certificates or certificates of participation in his area of responsibility. Think about it...

"Those Who Join You for Money, Will Also Leave You Again for Money" — Finding the Best Salespeople and Keeping Them

Choosing a sales team skillfully for work in the field or in-house and to lead them properly is the big challenge for managers today. No employee is closer to the customer, nobody can influence the turnover of your business faster and more sustainably then your salespeople!

At the same time the unemployment rate in Germany is growing steadily and the number of vacant positions is growing.

Added to that, salespeople do not have a very good image in our culture and those with high potential rather choose other jobs. Attracting talent is often too expensive, promoting and developing one's own young talent usually takes too long — the market and the competition do not wait!

Now for the good news: Yes, they do exist: the TOP salespeople! You only have to look at the right place, identify the best talents, induct them optimally and ensure that they stay with your business for the long term.

Your Salespeople Must Be Prepared to Work Hard for Eight Hours a Day. Everything Else We Will Teach Them

I was privileged to experience Reinhold Würth conducting an interview at a congress on Crete in 2001. A memorable experience. After the interview, we as participants could ask questions. My questions then were: "What conditions must a sales employee fulfil to be hired by you?" Answer: "They must be prepared to work hard for eight hours a day. Everything else we will teach them." Good. "And apart from that? Which other points are important?", I pushed on. After thinking for a short while Mr. Würth repeated: "Working hard for eight hours." Okay.

It took years until I understood this question properly. Only when I dealt more specifically with the term "management" in sales I realized what this response meant.

Reinhold Würth has decades-long sales experience. His company employs more than 33,000 employees in the field and it is very successful. He should know!

So what does his response mean then?

1. Marketing and sales can be learnt.

2. If employees stick to an appropriate system for sales, they will be successful.

3. For a manager, the core task is to find suitable employees for sales, to induct them, to manage them and to keep them.

If you have the responsibility for staff or management of sales, then I would gladly support you in your task to find suitable salespeople and to retain them.

We Could Grow Much More if We Had the Right Salespeople!

Are you a manager and this statement could have come from you? How does the next financial year look for you and your sales? What guides you when you think of turnover?

What is written in the media? Economic figures (according to which the growth of 0.7% this year would be lowered to 0.4% according to the forecast — which still means GROWTH!)?

The normal complaints in the industry? Or do you determine your own business cycle? You know already: "Bad times are good times for salespeople!"

One of my clients, a market-leading car bank, was looking for 75 new salespeople to work in the field in the crisis year 2009. The result of this can be seen in the business section of the daily newspaper: "Brand, market and leadership position in the market extended!"While the competition in my hometown is closing its factory, my client invests billions in the extension of his factory! Not only my business has had its best financial year in 2012, but so have many of my clients! But you know, this does not get spoken about so openly here in Germany.

And what is the biggest challenge for my clients (a total of 105 this year — so definitely representative) in sales in the coming year?

TIP

"We could grow much more if we had the right salespeople!"

That is what must be built on!

Can and Want to in The Swiss Army

A Swiss reserve officer once told me how soldiers are deployed optimally in an emergency.

Very simply put, the Swiss army differentiates between willingness to perform (lazy, hardworking) and capability to perform (clever, stupid) of the soldiers. The following logic emerges from this:

The stupid and lazy soldiers are deployed on the frontlines as "cannon fodder".

The stupid but hardworking soldiers are used as reinforcements behind the lines.

The clever and hardworking soldiers are almost all non-commissioned officers.

But the clever, lazy soldiers are officers. Why? Because they know that their energy, time and resources are limited and they have to deploy them optimally or intelligently.

;-)

What does this thought mean for sales?

TIP

Naturally, it is a basic value to be hardworking in sales, but it is even more important to act optimally or intelligently in sales. And here there are only two ways for managers: To (further) qualify existing employees and/or to hire new employees who "are there" already!

And where do you find these talents? How do you identify the best salespeople? How do you induct them and how do you retain your top people?

"Youths Research" and "Learning by Doing" With Sales — Please Don't!

Pilots at the German airline Lufthansa first have to go to Frankfurt for a few weeks to the flight simulator before they can fly a new type of airplane.

Soldiers are trained for weeks with a new weapon before they get deployed with it.

Yes, that costs a lot of money as well as time! But only this way can it be guaranteed that the requirements are met.

So how is it with salespeople? And here I am not even talking about the induction, the onboarding of new employees — I have written about this several times here already — I mean, how are salespeople prepared for selling a new product or providing a new service? In most cases the salesperson only gets brief training on the product, followed by the good wishes of the boss … and now turnover is supposed to kick in with the new product. And then everyone is surprised that the new product is not "accepted by the market"?

In order for a salesperson to make a new product successful from the start, the following conditions must be met:

Bulleted lists

- A list with the features of the product and the resulting benefits for the customer = so that a proper pitch can be made.

- Witnesses/referrals who can prove that the features and benefits really exist. Here different types of witnesses are important: The press, studies, referrals by customers, references etc. If you do not yet have enough witnesses, then you "create" some: articles are "placed" in the press, you "obtain" references with pilot projects… = convince the customer: You shorten the sales pitch drastically and provide maximum security for the customer.

- Should the innovation bring your customer more turnover or profit or when there is a cost saving, a prepared economic efficiency calculation is imperative. When doing this, do not only taker procurement costs into account, but also process costs! If you as a salesperson can show the benefits in numbers in the form of pencil selling, you are sure to succeed!

- A current, complete and clear comparison with the competition is useful if your customers are comparing your product with those of the competition. Be prepared!

- Determine which questions are useful when it comes to analyzing the requirements and needs of your customers in relation to the new product. Create a catalogue of questions and define the order of the questions which is tactically clever = Note: First establish the need, then argue precisely, point for point!

- Which pretexts and objections do you expect from your client? Draw up a list and of these and write down a solution for each. Now it's time to formulate the right answer with the appropriate conversation technique (flash, higher aim, self-correction, 180-degree method, etc.). Remember: You can write anything on paper! Learn your answers off by heart! Practice the wording so often, that it seems completely natural.

- What opportunities for additional sales are offered by the new solution? Have you got a strategy for up- and cross selling potential?

- What do you "show" your customer? Samples, newspaper clippings, brochures, photos… all of that has to be very well prepared = "A good salesman creates the pictures in the head of his customer!"

- And while we are talking about pictures: "Ten points you should look out for with…"… the checklist for "spiritual arson" makes sense right from the beginning. Remember that some products only work with the purchase motives "pain and fear"!

Picasso said: "A man who does not prepare for his chance only has himself to blame!" Naturally, this also applies to women and salespeople who go to customers unprepared! "One shot only"… when your first attempt seems amateurish to the customer, it will be difficult to get the customer to accept the new product after that!

So who should prepare the "homework" above? Well…, I see product development, product management and marketing as "service provider" for the sales department. But in the end, it is teamwork from all participants.

That reminds me: During my "former life", when I was on the road as trade representative, I always had the support of both product managers. On the first day of the trade fair they would collect all the information of the products and the terms and conditions of the competition. Overnight these data would be prepared on an Excel spreadsheet and given to me during breakfast. All the advantages and disadvantages would be highlighted in different colors, so that the list was self-explanatory. In this way I was prepared for all pretexts and objections of my customers: Nobody could tell me that the competition was "better" regarding their product or their terms and conditions. And should it be indeed so… I was prepared!

Yes, the list was not 100% complete… but if a salesperson starts off with this sort of preparation when introducing a new product, they will clearly be much more successful! Guaranteed! And by the way: Your customers will also be happy when the salesperson can provide concrete details about his offer from

the start!

LEARNING

The saying goes that if you do not want to improve daily, you will not be good in the long term. In our current fast-paced world we constantly need to develop further, personally as well as with our professional skills as salespeople and managers. And learning can be fun! Regarding fun: On the following pages you will get insights into my idea of inspiring learning.

Stupid! This Is Not From My Field. I Can Learn Nothing There!
Great! This Is Not From My Field. There I Can Learn a Lot!

Weekend. Enduro driver course. Nine men and one trainer. But I am actually a motocross guy. Fast bends, high jumps, prepared circuit. Enduro: The guys who drive through the forest with lights on their motorbike, trying to overcome the obstacles posed by nature. Let's see what I can learn from them. After all, I can only get better.

Motocross and enduro. This is like soccer and handball. Or downhill and cross-country skiing. The tools are similar, yet different. In sport it is common to compare yourself with other disciplines. What can I learn from this for me, for my discipline?

What is this like in business? In marketing and sales?

One gets participants who say they have learnt nothing from a presentation as the speaker is not from their industry: "So many examples from the sale of products. But we only provide services!"

Excuse me? No, no! If you turn it around, this would mean: I cannot learn anything from enduro racers because they have a light on their motorcycle?!

With what attitudes do participants go to such an event? "Find everything that does not work for us" or "find everything, that can make us even more successful?" Your focus determines your success!

For his stage performance as bodybuilder Arnold Schwarzenegger hired a ballet teacher. The American military stages maneuvers with its allies. The freight specialists from DHL travelled a year with the Formula 1 teams to observe their logistics processes. And participants say: "There were not enough examples from my field?" Ok.

So with which attitude and with which viewpoint do you attend presentations and seminars? What is your focus when you read professional literature? Where do you get new ideas from to be more successful in sales?

If you only look around in your own industry, you can only copy the competition. That will never make you number one in your field! You will always just walk in the footsteps of the competition!

Look for other businesses, industries and people from whom you can learn!

The successful hotelier Klaus Kobjoll is a fantastic example for the subject of recruiting and leadership. The hairdresser Albert Bachmann is a benchmark for optimal positioning from the viewpoint of the customer. Gustav Naujoks, who is involved with a metalworking business in Bavaria, has optimized his purchasing process to such an extent, that I gape in astonishment!

Have a good look! Be receptive to what is out there!

The Other Day, Sitting on the Couch With My Love …

We are looking at the fish in the new aquarium. She says: "The two males are courting the female." Ok, I just see fish swimming around wildly.

I will admit, I know what type of fish I will order in a Sushi restaurant, but I don't know much more about these animals. But I have outstanding knowledge about salespeople and conducting conversations! In return, my love can often listen to my analysis of the daily situation: "Have you heard his customer referral? Just a pity that he defended the referral when the customer had already rejected him. And then he still missed two definite signals to purchase!"

Why do I write about this? Because I am convinced that salespeople can only develop further if they consciously study sales techniques.

A good salesperson is not necessarily the one who concludes many sales. Sometimes there are also conditions which cannot be influenced directly.

For me, the decisive factor is whether the salesperson, after having met a customer, can explain exactly why he has concluded the sale or why he was not able to make a sale. What he should have done to be successful.

You can also sharpen your senses for a good sales technique in many everyday situations: in the cinema during a good movie, at a discussion on TV, at a sermon in a church service or with salespeople who want to sell you something. Have a good look and learn to analyze the situation correctly.

Many years ago, a national soccer player was the guest on the German sports TV show *Aktuelles Sportstudio*. Because the player had scored so many goals, the presenter asked him why he was so successful in kicking goals. The player got up, swung his kicking leg and pretended to shoot a goal. "I do it like this!" were his words as he sat down again. For a moment, the presenter and the audience were irritated. But then many of them laughed and applauded.

But the soccer player was totally serious!

My interpretation: This soccer player will not still significantly improve his performance, as he does not know how to. And as a trainer the man would completely fail, as he would not be able to tell other players how to improve. The expert term is: »Unconscious competence« = you are good, but you don't know why.

"We do not have too little time, we have too much time which we don't use."

Lucius Annaeus Seneca

I earn my money with knowledge and skill. Just like most salespeople. At the same time, I am always expected to be innovative and to have advanced knowledge in my profession. Sure! So how do I manage to identify as much of the latest know how as possible? Here is my personal solution:

1. I read a lot. Especially current magazines and professional journals. For this I have a dozen subscriptions: *Psychologie heute, Internet World Business, Wirtschaftswoche, Harvard Business Manager* and many more…

2. Book summaries from *Get Abstract*. I also like audio summaries: Within 10 minutes I know whether a book is useful for me or not! Genius! One hour of walking training = six book summaries!

3. Audio books and the sound track of DVDs. Mostly on long car trips. When it is possible for me to listen to a book rather than to read it, then the audio format is the most time-saving version for me!

4. I only buy the hard copy version of a book when I find the audiobook exciting. I then work through this with a marker pen and a notepad.

5. If an audiobook is not available, I have to read the actual book…

And when I occasionally do not feel like professional material? Then I recommend my three favorite audiobook authors: Nicholas Sparks, Daniel Glattauer und Paulo Coelho.

Do you know that most books bought in Germany are not read right to the end?

Mud, Sand and Clay — Fulfil Your Dreams!

I remember that I could ride a motorbike before I could ride a bicycle. With the bicycle I initially had the problem that the pedals always made me lose my balance. And because my father was a fanatical motorbike rider at the time, I had a 50ccm children's machine standing in the garage "by pure chance". Later on, I had an enduro for the road, but this one mostly just stood in a corner. Leisure time stress!

My resolution for 2012 was to make a dream of mine come true: I have always wanted to fly meters high through the air with a motocross bike. Motocross has always fascinated me!

Said and done! Since May I regularly drive through mud, sand and clay. My skills as a rider are slightly above those of a novice. At the age of 44 I experience ten-year-olds racing past me. This is an exciting experience! It is so much fun. It poses a big challenge for one's physique and for one's coordination and the high jumps are pure adrenalin! Wow!

After I tried to teach myself the riding technique in the beginning, I saw after a few training hours that I would not have progressed by myself! On the contrary: I was busy teaching myself a wrong riding technique.

I therefore booked some training hours and signed up for different rider technique courses. The result: I am making significant progress with my development as motocross rider and I enjoy training with others.

In a group especially, I push my boundaries to the limit and beyond. And when I compare myself to the other riders, I can see that I am not the only one making certain mistakes, and that is reassuring.

Why do I tell you this?

1. Fulfill your dreams! One day it will be too late for your dream! Do not wait too long!

2. Regularly find a task where you are a beginner. Learn something completely new. This way you learn a lot about yourself and it gives you a good opportunity to think about your actions.

3. Look for a training partner and a coach. And this brings us to the topic of sales and acquisition.

I Am Practical, I Do Not Read Books!

I am constantly looking for new trainers for my team. By doing this, I have interesting experiences:

An applicant, in answering my question in a telephonic interview about the last book she has read about the subject of sales and marketing, said: "I do not read books. I am practical."

Hmmm… that is what she says to me! To me, someone who writes books himself and who has every relevant publication on the subject in his bookshelf! To me, who spends hours every week reading professional literature!

Another applicant told me with deep conviction that "one" either has "it" or not. He has been successful in marketing for years, he said. He knows what it takes. According to him, he really did not think that he needs to be educated as a trainer. He knew how "one" makes sales.

On the evening of our telephonic interview he had just finished attending a two-day sales seminar to which he was "sent" by his current employer. When I asked him what insight he had gained from the training session, he explained that he felt that the seminar was probably something for beginners. He could not really find anything inspiring for himself there.

I probably do not have to mention that these two candidates did not make it any further in the selection process. But what lies behind these statements that should make us as salespeople think?

"Man has three ways to act wisely. First of all by thinking: that is the most noble. Secondly by imitating: that is the easiest. Thirdly through experience: that is the hardest." This is a quote from Confucius.

Contained in this is the hint, that imitating, copying and modelling are the easiest and often also the quickest ways to success. Our children set the example: They copy our behavior.

That is quite normal. And books play a special role in this. By reading a book in my professional field, I can profit very specifically from the experiences of the author. Of course there are other options of imitating, but books have a very special place here.

When last have you read a book about the subject of sales and marketing? And even more important: From what you have read: is there something you have at least tried in your daily business?

For the second applicant three remarks come to mind:
First, the parable of the master and his pupil, who does not make any progress with learning. The master puts a full glass of water into the hand of the pupil and then still pours another half a liter of water into the glass which is already full. Everything overflows and becomes a puddle on the ground. The pupil tells the master that there is no space for the water as the glass is already full, to which the master replies: "That is true. And you are — in the same way the glass is full of water and nothing else

can fit into it — full of knowledge, prejudices, beliefs and habits and you will learn nothing from me until you are prepared to get rid of the old to make space for the new!"

What have you learnt lately? Are you open to new ideas or do you often think: "Great idea — but we won't do that"?

Second insight: It is clear, and not only since the two best-sellers "Outliers" and "The Talent Code" hit the shelves last year: People are not born with target-orientated communication — and selling is nothing else but that! The statement that as a salesperson "one" just has "it" or not is therefore complete nonsense! If this was so, all seminars, coaching sessions and training programs as well as having trainers for salespeople would be unnecessary!

Third insight: The American management guru Tom Peters wants to have this inscription on his gravestone: "He was curious to the end." I like that. I urge you to also stay inquisitive until the end! Learn throughout your life!

TIP

Wise people think that their knowledge is a drop in the ocean. Uneducated people think they know everything already!

Or as Steve Jobs says: Stay hungry. Stay foolish.

Further Education with a Hit Rate of 21%? — Please No!

Can a walk over hot coals make a team stick together? Can further training lead employees to more success? Can one learn how to master crises in life in an evening workshop and change your personal self completely? Hardly. That is the sobering result of a study of the Institute for Applied Sciences e.V. (iaw-Köln). Two thirds of those surveyed in the study stated that they could not notice "any positive and sustainable changes." Although employees like participating in further training, only 21% believe that the training led to some improvement.

A few weeks ago, I discovered this text on the internet. I could hardly stop shaking my head when reading this...

That makes me think of a saying: "You do not go out and HAVE a great life, you go out and CREATE a great life!"

What is our inner attitude towards the subject of further education? Surely this is not something that just happens to us! It surely is a process that happens within us. We do not get educated further, we educate ourselves further! Active rather than passive. Acting instead of reacting. Debt to be collected instead of debt to be brought.

The statements of those surveyed can be compared very nicely with what new members of a fitness studio say at this time of the year: "I have been a member in the fitness studio for over a month now and still cannot see any progress!" Hmm — how about training, sweating, suffering, overcoming yourself... being subscribed as a member is not quite enough!

The comparison fits!

Yes, a walk over hot coals at a seminar over the weekend can result in a big change in one's life. The same applies to presentations, day seminars, coaching, books films etc.

To all managers amongst the readers here: Don't waste your money on further training if you have employees with the attitude as described earlier on. Those are expenses, not investments. And none of the participants enjoy it. Also not the presenters, speakers, trainers, teachers and coaches. Either you manage to change the attitude of your employees about this subject, or you should ask yourself whether you really have the right employees with whom you want to celebrate future successes!

Another two comments about this:

1. Seminars are only tools for further education. Books, DVDs, audiobooks, coaching sessions, sponsor and mentor programs are also good tools! It depends on what you want to achieve with your training.

2. Yes, there are big qualitative differences between speakers. And just because you once had a bad speaker does not imply that all presenters are bad! Compare.

Cheat Sheets for Salespeople — or: Success Does Not Have to Happen by Chance

Do you know Jordan Belfort? He is the main character in *The Wolf of Wall Street*. Do you know how this man earns his money nowadays? He gives lectures about his experiences in business and … he writes sales guides: Companies pay Jordan 50,000 dollars a day to provide them with a suitable line of argumentation!

And I keep on discussing the use of conversation guides with salespeople and managers!?

Let me formulate a few thoughts about this:

1. Selling is a trade that has little or nothing to do with talent. Therefore, most people can learn it. If you want to! "The most important thing when selling is that you learn to read from a script so that it does not sound as if you are reading from a script. [...] Just pretend you are an actor on a stage: You pitch your voice high and then bring it down again; you speak faster and then slower again. This way you keep your customers interested and ensure that they listen to you attentively. And don't even think about picking up the phone until you have answers to all conceivable objections." (Jordan Belfort)

2. Yes, I also know them, the call center agents (no, they are not salespeople), who want to sell me something by reading a text to me. Everyone notices straight away that they read something off a script. But we as potential buyers expect more!

We want to be convinced. We want to sense a genuine interest in us and our needs. We want to believe that our counterpart is convinced of what he offers us! Otherwise we won't buy anything and just feel harassed. So: Salespeople should not read off a script at all! And learning a script off by heart (badly) is also not acceptable at all!

3. Pablo Picasso once said: "A man who does not prepare for his chance only has himself to blame!" By the way, I do think that this also applies to women! So, we prepare for an examination. Mostly by making notes: "Thinking on paper". Maybe we also prepare a crib note. And most of the time we don't need it after all. Either we have internalized the knowledge by now or we risk being caught cheating. But: We do prepare!

   Before important telephone conversations, I draft a plan for myself. In writing. For me it would be fatal if I would "forget" topics, questions and arguments which I really wanted to raise in the conversation.

4. Success in sales has little to do with chance! It is well known that certain speech patterns, questions, lines of arguments, examples, stories, rhetorical pictures and formulations are more effective than others when it comes to sales! There are certain "magic words" that trigger a decision to make a purchase in your counterpart. If this is so, then it is not necessary for each salesperson to reinvent the wheel for every sales conversation. They can stick to what has so often worked in the past! Create a standard for your argument and stick to it. You only have to be creative when you formulate your guide-

line. After that it is all about perfectly implementing your chosen strategy.

> "We wanted our salespeople to be young, naïve, hungry and stupid. [...] Give me someone like that and I will make them rich without any problems. But if you give me somebody with intelligence and an imagination — well, that will be a bit more difficult."
>
> *Jordan Belfort*

5. A thought for managers: It is your job to create standards and systems! This applies to the line of argumentation and the way conversations are conducted by your salespeople!

   Stop relying on sales where a few talented people are responsible for your turnover and move to system sales, where a whole team brings in business. Würth calls this: "Win the game with your pawns!" With system sales you might not have the best eleven players, but you have the best team of eleven!

   So... create standards!

6. A second thought for managers: Currently and in the future, the biggest challenge is finding new salespeople. Salespeople that just have it!

With appropriate standards, you can make cuts in the selection process, have a shorter training period and have to lead less tightly.

To the point: Sales managers who do not create standards are in the wrong job!

- And now in practice: What can you do? What do I recommend for you?

- In my team we do not have previously set guidelines: Every salesperson writes their own script in their own "language" in their own way according to my philosophy and my standards. In this way I avoid acceptance problems in the team.

- Scripts are never running texts, but always keywords only: With a running text there is always the temptation to just read it off! Keywords can be used much more spontaneously and in a flexible way. That makes a much better impression on the customer.

- Certain phrases are important: Getting started, assessing the need, reasoning, preparing and dealing with objections, conclusion. Clear standards, minimal creativity.

- "Practice makes perfect!" Practice, practice, practice!

- My trainers and I often sit and listen in. During days in the office we normally sit around the same table with the salespeople. By doing this we can constantly give feedback and celebrate successes together.

The Mathematical Game Theory for Doctors and the Law of Effect

"A salesperson that is good in a personal interview and can be convincing there, is not necessarily good with telephonic communication! But a salesperson that can be convincing on the telephone, is normally also good in a personal conversation!"

Sure, that is a claim, a thesis. But there is something to it, because:

in 1967 an Israeli research team investigated the effect of communication and came to the following findings: The share of what is received by the counterpart during personal communication (for example when the field worker advises customers during a visit) is conveyed up to 55% by the person's presence: clothing, attitude, eye contact, body language, mimicry, gestures. appearance. The way in which something is said, counts for up to 38%: voice, modulation, volume, tempo. Words only count for 7% when it comes to making a decision.

During a telephonic conversation, the 55% conveyed by personal presence fall away. Here the distribution looks like this:

TIP

"What" is said counts for 12% and 88% "how" it is said.

This is the reason why many salespeople like to avoid the sales or acquisition talk by telephone and rather do cold calling.

(Mehrabian, Albert & Susan R. Ferris, *Inference of attitudes from nonverbal communication in two channels*, Journal of Consulting Psychology S. 252.)

But even more impressive is the story of Dr. Fox, who held a lecture on the subject of "Mathematic game theory for doctors" at the University of Southern California School of Medicine in 1970. The whole audience of medical students was enthused by his lecture. Many did not expect anything different, as they had read some of his work beforehand and because Dr. Fox was already known as an expert in this subject area.

What is impressive about this example is that Dr. Fox is not an expert on the subject he talks about, but he has gained this reputation because of the way he says things! Three psychologists engaged an actor to give a lecture during which he was not allowed to build one sentence on the other. It was stipulated that not a single sentence should make sense — during the lecture as well as in the round of questions that followed afterwards. That was a real challenge for the actor "Dr. Fox".

With this experiment psychologists proved that even a professional audience can be inspired by a lecture totally devoid of content.

Unbelievable? Then see the experiment for yourself. You can find this audio recording from 1970 on my YouTube channel.

Conclusion: This shows that it is not enough to have your well thought out text prepared, in today's jargon, your "wording"!

Your own attitude is far more important, as it does not only determine your tone in the conversation but also determines your body language.

The Home Trainer for New Customers

A few weeks ago, Professor Dr. Knoblauch and I held a roadshow across Germany: five days, five cities, five times the same content. In direct alternation and daily from 09:00 a.m. to 05:00 p.m., the theme was "Finding the best salespeople and keeping them".

And here are the fascinating insights: On which seminar days did I make the most notes? When did I have the most lightbulb moments?

On the fifth and last day of the seminars!

On the fifth seminar day? Now you might ask yourself whether I am a bit slow perhaps?

For me it especially thrilling to read books more than once, to listen to audio books over and over again, to watch DVDs a few times over and to sometimes repeat a seminar.

Why? Obviously — content and information are better internalized through repetition.

That is why I started buying seminars as DVD sets years ago. On my shelf I have, for example, the DVDs of Bodo Schäfer, Dr Oliver Pott, Alex S. Rusch and many more. With these I use my time in a targeted way during long journeys to educate myself further.

EPILOG

"Selective perception is a psychological phenomenon, in which only certain aspects of the environment are perceived and others are disregarded. Selective perception is based on the skill to recognize patterns — a basic mechanism of the human brain. The brain is constantly looking for patterns in order to better add new information to that which is already present. Thereby selective perception is a — mostly subconscious — search for a certain pattern. This is necessary in order to even be able to manage the huge amount of information," according to Wikipedia.

If you have read the book until here, you will know my own preferred patterns of perception: Sales, marketing, management and motivation. Maybe now I am able to move your perception filter a bit more into that direction as well. Everyday life is full of good ideas for salespeople and their managers! Use the suggestions and use them in practice... I would be sad if what you said at the end of this book was: "Great idea — but not for us!"

In this sense I would like to wish you a "good catch" always and look forward to hopefully meeting you personally at one of my events.

Yours
Dirk Kreuter

About Dirk Kreuter

Dirk Kreuter is not only one of the most sought-after speakers in the German-speaking world, but also Europe's #1 sales trainer.

In over 50 specialist books, DVDs and audio books, which are also available internationally, you will receive the know-how of the sales expert in a multimedia format.

For example, Dirk Kreuter's book *Umsatz Extrem* [Extreme Sales] landed on *Manager Magazine's* bestseller list.

Dirk Kreuter coaches more than 79,000 companies and 121,000 self-employed individuals from the German-speaking medium-sized enterprise sector. More than 40,000 participants attend his seminars annually, and more than 60,000 people participated in digital events hosted by him in 2021.

Photo: Inka Englisch

Facts about Dirk Kreuter

Dirk Kreuter is successful in many ways. He is a businessman with over 150 employees at locations in Bochum, Hannover, Dubai & Singapore. As an investor, he is active in 9 company investments and had a volume of 44 million euros in 2021, 80 million euros in 2022, and his goal for 2023 is to increase the volume to 140 million euros.

Aside from his successful entrepreneurship, he is also an author and has published over 100 books, audiobooks, and online courses. His book "Umsatz Extrem" was on the bestseller list of the Manager Magazine. Since 2018, over 500,000 copies of his bestseller "Decision: Success" have been sold. With "Bestseller Training," he offers the largest German-language online course on sales and leadership with over 1,000 videos.

Dirk is also a speaker and mentor and has given inspiring speeches and seminars in 16 countries in German and English since 1990. He is also a Certified Speaking Professional (CSP). His podcasts with over 1,000 episodes and 22+ million downloads earned him the Tiger Award in 2017-2018.

As a Youtuber, he has published over 3,000 videos, 1,100 of which are publicly accessible, and has 120,000 subscribers and 44+ million views (gross).

He has over 24,000 sales and affiliate partners and is a leading provider in Europe for seminars on "Sales and Sales" with more than 40,000 registrations per year at his event "Sales Offensive."

He even holds the world record for the largest sales training (Guinness Book 2018) in the Dortmund Westfalenhalle.

MASTER-OF-SALES

**A 6-month program for
the self-employed and entrepreneurs.**

✓ Positioning your own brand correctly

✓ Pricing and creating the right offer

✓ Winning qualified inquiries by becoming visible
to your ideal customers

✓ Sales training: consistently closing deals with
your ideal customers by handling objections and
recognizing buyer signals

✓ Becoming visible with online marketing;
direct access and technical training with
Dirk Kreuter's team

✓ 5 different weekly live calls with the experts
from the Dirk Kreuter team on the topics:
online marketing, paid PPC advertising, sales,
mindset, and copywriting

Product only available in German. English versions coming out soon.

MASTER-OF-SALES CONSULTING

A 12-month program for entrepreneurs

✓ Evaluating current positioning and offers
(finding opportunities)

✓ Scaling an existing offer the right way
(like Dirk, but with a sparring partner by your side)

✓ Breaking through plateaus

✓ Finding, hiring, and retaining the right employees
(through digitalization and optimization
of processes)

✓ Leadership in the company

✓ Weekly live calls with the experts from
Dirk Kreuter's team on the topics: online
marketing, paid PPC advertising, sales,
mindset and copywriting

Product only available in German. English versions coming out soon.

DIGITAL SYSTEM
SALES SOLUTION

Mixture of a pre-recorded e-learning system and a program for entrepreneurs with annual sales of €500,000 or more who want to digitalize their sales. Duration: 12 months

- ✓ Standardization of internal sales processes

- ✓ Digitalization and automation of internal sales processes

- ✓ Entirely thought out and ready-to-go sales training by Dirk Kreuter for your sales department to achieve maximum results in the shortest possible time. Implemented directly on the platform

- ✓ Internal e-learning platform with control over learning inventory and 100% control over content and modules. Independent expansion is possible

- ✓ Sales recruiting, onboarding and leadership

- ✓ Key performance indicators in sales

Product only available in German. English versions coming out soon.

MASTERMIND

'THIS IS WHERE MARKET LEADERS ARE CREATED'

The best network for the medium-sized entrepreneur in search of the right environment. More than 100 active members. Exchanges, partnerships and fun in the collective.

- ✓ More than 100 active members

- ✓ Meet 4 times a year in the best hotels and work together, network and exchange ideas (Dubai, Switzerland - 2 to 4 days each)

- ✓ Different expert panels at every meeting

- ✓ Knowledge exchange without taboos (Dirk Kreuter and participants share their secrets, NDA must be signed upon admission)

- ✓ Includes access to all seminars and events by Dirk Kreuter

- ✓ Direct access to Dirk Kreuter personally via WhatsApp

- ✓ Access to Dirk Kreuter's network

Product only available in German. English versions coming out soon.

MY LEARNINGS

1. _______________________________

2. _______________________________

3. _______________________________

4. _______________________________

5. _______________________________

6. _______________________________

7. _______________________________

8. _______________________________

9. _______________________________

10. ______________________________

MY LEARNINGS

1. ______________________________

2. ______________________________

3. ______________________________

4. ______________________________

5. ______________________________

6. ______________________________

7. ______________________________

8. ______________________________

9. ______________________________

10. ______________________________